A Self- Love Story

30 Day Guide to Self Love
and Emotional Healing

SHUNTA L WILBORN

BALBOA.
PRESS
A DIVISION OF HAY HOUSE

Balboa Press books may be ordered through booksellers or by contacting:

Balboa Press
A Division of Hay House
1663 Liberty Drive
Bloomington, IN 47403
www.balboapress.com
1 (877) 407-4847

Print information available on the last page.

ISBN: 978-1-9822-2984-9 (sc)
ISBN: 978-1-9822-2985-6 (e)

Balboa Press rev. date: 08/13/2019

Contents

In the Beginning...

"The best day of your life is the one on which you decide your life is your own. No apologies or excuses. No one to lean on, rely on, or blame. The gift is yours - it is an amazing journey - and you alone are responsible for the quality of it. This is the day your life really begins."

- BOB MOAWAD

I've decided to create a self-love mantra, as the start of a love affair I intend to have with myself. While I certainly love myself, I must admit that I have not demonstrated the deeply intimate unconditional love that I give so easily to others. I have a sneaky suspicion I am not alone.

Like many, self-worth and self-acceptance are areas I have allowed to go under developed; funny how we do not care for ourselves with the same intensity that we care for our friends and family members. Often, our personal wellbeing is shifted to the bottom of our very long to-do lists, neglected for what we think are more pressing issues. The truth is, a lack of attention to our personal needs leaves us lost and depleted of the happiness we so desperately desire.

I have made a personal commitment to 30 days of developing habits of loving and prioritizing myself. This journey will involve self-care, albeit something much more than bubble baths and me time. I intend to create an environment where my needs are more important than anyone or anything else. On the surface that sounds extremely selfish, but…so what if it is?! We have no problem giving in to the selfish demands of others we love and care for. Why not honor ourselves in the same way, indulging our own selfish desires? I've decided I can and I will. I am worth it.

If you are like me, it can feel a bit unnatural to say, "I love myself". I intend to explore and address these feelings starting today! It is important for me to shine a light into the shadows and fall in love with everything that is uniquely me. Saying, "I love myself" should feel empowering, liberating, like freedom! But for many it feels untrue. This, in my opinion, is the deepest betrayal of self and misuse of love.

Self-love is the most important gift you can offer yourself. I understand that what I project into the Universe about myself is graciously given back to me, multiplied. Only, it cannot be manipulated. I intend to uncover the root of any unflattering views I have about myself and manifest the beautiful expressions of life that are uniquely me.

If ever you have felt desperate to experience unconditional and uncompromising love, now is a great time to create a personal "self-love" mantra of your own. As your self-acceptance deepens it's okay that the mantra expand and evolve. In fact it should. Ultimately, you have within yourself everything you need to live a physically and emotionally loving and expansive life.

For the next 30 days, join me as I focus on loving and accepting myself more each day. My goal is to become unapologetically me! I want to show up for myself. I want to love myself unconditionally and without regard for the approval or validation of others.

Here is my "Self-Love" mantra. Prayerfully, it will inspire you to create one of your own and begin the most significant journey of your life.

My Mantra for Self-Love and Self-Acceptance

I love myself. I offer myself the gift of unconditional love and acceptance. I receive it freely. I give myself permission to explore life in a way that is exciting and feeds my needs. I believe that everything I need to live happily is effortlessly given to me by the loving Universe. I am free to choose and create loving experiences for myself. I am a delightful person and those who recognize my awesomeness are drawn to me. The Universe supports my decision to deepen my love for myself.

Day One Reflection

_____

_____

_____

_____

_____

_____

_____

_____

_____

_____

_____

_____

_____

_____

_____

_____

_____

_____

_____

_____

_____

_____

Shunta L Wilborn

Day Two: The Pursuit

"Step into the fire of self-discovery. This fire will not burn you, it will only burn what you are not."

-Mooji

During my bath tonight, I listened to a YouTube lecture by the late pastor Dr. Myles Monroe entitled, "Keys to Self-Love". In it, Dr. Monroe discussed seven key strategies for developing a stronger relationship with yourself. His idea of a pursuit of singleness (relationship with ones' self) as a means to self-knowledge, self-acceptance, and self-love resonated deeply with me. Dr. Monroe's words reminded me that the need to be loved is most efficiently satisfied through personal discovery. The path to deeper, more fulfilling relationships begin when we discover and nurture the truth that we are.

Self-discovery and mastery have become my highest priority. It feels empowering to search my inner self for the answers. As I did tonight, I intend to use books or lectures as tools only, understanding that they provide truth diluted by someone else's perspective. Following guidance from an outside source can be beneficial but feels like a shallow substitute for the inner guidance that knows me intimately and loves me completely. After all, the most important person I should desire to know and love is me.

If you ask the average person if they love themselves, they will emphatically respond "yes". But the truth is, most people don't. In fact, they know very little about themselves, unable to express in any depth who they are, aside from the apparent.

When you love someone you want to be more than just acquainted. You're excited to experience life through that person's eyes. You want to know their character, qualities and nature. You're interested to find out what they like, what makes them happy, what they enjoy and what displeases them. Sadly, few take the time to get to know themselves intimately, never exploring those mysterious yet intriguing parts of their personal character. They find it easier to create an identity based on superficial personal observations or even worse, on the perceptions and opinions of someone else.

Dr. Monroe's lecture has empowered me to explore my personal habits as they relate to loving myself and others. What I discovered was a bit unsettling. I realized that I tend to offer love, both platonically and intimately, as a means to receive it. I extend uncompromising affection to others even when it is obviously unwanted or undeserved. I disregard all of the warning signs and move single-mindedly towards my goal of getting my emotional needs met. Not only is this a form of manipulation, it is a direct path to heartache and disappointment.

Today, I give up the need to have anyone else love me. Understanding that no one can know or love me to the degree that I can. That's not to say that a loving relationship is off the radar. My point is simply that it's no longer necessary for my happiness.

I am finding that a personal love affair is a critical part of my emotional healing. My expanding love for myself alleviates the desire to solicit others to satisfy my emotional cravings. I understand in a practical way that the needy energy we project can never be truly satisfied by anything outside of ourselves. In fact, that hunger for someone else's attention is sure to attract the wrong people and wrong opportunities into our lives. We all want and deserve satisfying relationships, however dependency on someone else to meet our needs is both unhealthy and dangerous. When we become the object of our own attention, there is no deficit to be compensated for if and when someone takes theirs away.

It feels liberating to say that the most important person for me to love is me. Not my husband, my children, my parents…it's me. As a woman who loves her family deeply, the idea of putting myself first was not easily accepted. It felt selfish and unnatural. Society has trained women especially, to esteem the needs of others above our own, misleading us into unfulfilled lives and dysfunctional families. The truth is, when we neglect ourselves, everything and everyone else suffers. Love is a meaningful exchange that flows from the inside out.

Dr. Monroe also addressed self-love as it relates to self-identity and source. According to Monroe, discovering your source - where you come from - directly impacts how well you love yourself.

He made the analogy of a diamond and plastic ring. He asked, if you were given both, which would you love more? Which would you esteem and protect? The obvious answer here is the diamond. Why? Because of its origin; it is considered more valuable. Plastic rings are common; they can be acquired anyplace. Not the case for diamonds.

Monroe's point is that the Divine Creator is our source. Love for ourselves should be relative to the love and value that we give to our God. We are made in the image and likeness of God so we too, are divine creators. Acceptance of our divine nature directly influences self-worth, esteem, concept, identity, value, and most importantly, our self-love.

Monroe's words reminded me that I determine my value, my opinion is what matters. So much so, that I've decided not to ask anyone else's opinion about anything for at least the next 7 days. I feel empowered to make some drastic and lasting changes. I'm excited to trust my instincts alone.

Reclaiming my power, I am free to be me. I love and esteem myself and my own opinion above anyone else's. I want to go deeper into this exploration of who I really am and what I want my life to be. According to Dr. Monroe, the best way to do this is to rely on my source and not something outside of myself. I am an extension of source energy, the creator of all that is. I get my value from that source and I am excited to see where this takes me.

Today's Affirmation: I am a one-of-a-kind treasured asset!!

Day Two Reflection

_____

_____

_____

_____

_____

_____

_____

_____

_____

_____

_____

_____

_____

_____

_____

_____

_____

_____

_____

Shunta L Wilborn

Day Three: Taking Off the Masks

Wearing a mask wears you out. Faking it is fatiguing.
The most exhausting activity is pretending to be
what you know you aren't.

— Rick Warren

I spent time today re-reading Eckhart Tolle's book, "A New Earth". In Chapter 4, Tolle does an excellent job of explaining how we play pre-established roles that keep us from the authentic relationships we are so desperate to experience. I found his point of view even more insightful as I applied it to enhancing this new love relationship I am exploring with myself.

According to Tolle, authenticity is a foundation of power. Taking off social masks as he calls it, has freed me to expose the best parts of who I am. It feels like the beginning of my personal flowering so to speak. Often, we get stuck in that budding phase of life, never allowing our authentic selves to blossom. The light that we are is dimmed by our shadow selves and social roles that we exchange for authenticity. And while we may be afraid to show others who we really are, we are just as afraid to know what lies beneath our surface selves.

Taking off the social mask, abandoning the roles, looking myself square in the eyes and honestly saying, "I love who you are at this very moment", has been a life changing experience. Regardless of the mistakes I've made and stripped of the false self, I honor the person that looks back at me in the mirror. No longer will I bury my authentic self and allow an identity crafted in social trends and other peoples' opinions to thrive. Instead of fearing judgement and rejection. I accept my uniqueness as my power!

I am beginning to recognize my authentic self and I like her! Shunta, carefree and living according to her desires. Living fearlessly, one who doesn't have it all figured out. I am learning to follow my inner guidance and allow the chips to fall where they may. No longer afraid to be honest about my needs, I am determined to live the life I desire, not the life I settled for.

My developing identity urges me to explore love more deeply. What is love and why is self-love so important? Love is often associated with action. But is love really action? I think it can be, but not necessarily so. Love, I am learning, is a state of being. It just is, authentic and perfect, without need for anything else to enhance or define it. I am a reflection of that divine love. Love that is sure and creative, powerful and free. It is my identity, not something I feel as an emotion but what I experience as me. This means that sometimes it's happy and joyous and sometimes it's not. Sometimes it is angry and confused and hurt; this is certainly not many people's definition of love. We tend to only recognize love as that euphoric feeling we get when things are exactly the way we want them to be. What about when things are anxious, or nervous, or fearful? Am I no longer an expression of the Divine? Am I not one with God in those moments? Isn't she always there expressing herself through me?

Love has to be whatever I am, whenever, and self-love is accepting this truth. Owning the truth of who I am is a freedom that allows me to transform and transcend. Lately, I've felt the pull to explore this truth more deeply. If I am honest, I'm curious to know what that truth really feels like and I'm apprehensive of what I will find deep within myself as I have relied so heavily on things outside of myself to shape my definition of self and love.

I've decided not to consider how I have loved others nor use this information as a guideline for loving myself. My experiences are significant, but irrelevant right now. I really want to excavate a love from within that is unique and experienced by me alone.

So far, this journey has been more than satisfying, it feels empowering. I feel like my emotions are settled and my life energy is powerfully creating my desires. I don't experience any deficiency in self-assessment. No matter the situation it really is okay. There is perfection in every perceived imperfect circumstance. When I am sidetracked by intrusive, fearful thoughts, I bring my attention back to the love that is expanding inside me and this redirection helps center and disarm any feelings of inadequacy.

I remind myself often that I accept my divinity. This means I've activated the God force that I am. I command the circumstance of both my thoughts and actions; because God is Love, love is ultimately what I am. It is love that creates and sustains all good things, so in loving myself I create and sustain good things through my being. I have command over my emotions and the Universe is an extension of my being. I get to create loving experiences by expressing outwardly the love that is within. My life is love, manifested. It is most certainly the foundation of health, wealth, as well as my mental, emotional and physical wellbeing.

Tomorrow, I will be mindful to keep my inner dialogue loving. Careful not to be scolding or judgmental. I understand that what I say to myself directly affects the level of love that I allow myself to experience. I understand that the love is not created, it just is. It is either allowed to flow freely or it is resisted. My intention is to allow love to flow so powerfully that it is evident to everyone that I encounter. No more critical self-talk; I will no longer say negative things about myself, I refuse to. If there are things that I want to change I will focus on the positivity of the change and not the fact that there is something less than desirable needing to be changed. I will choose uplifting thoughts to help me while I make those changes. I can and will only think in a positive manner about myself and those that are important to me.

I will not overreact to missteps or mistakes. These things happen and most often they help us, showing up to help clarify for us what we really want in life. I am determined to appreciate every situation for assisting and supporting me on my journey.

I will focus on the things I desire and what I think those things will bring me. The answers to my questions form the catalyst to discovering the meaning of life's desires. Why do I want success? I want success because I want a deeper feeling of satisfaction, accomplishment, and influence. Why do I desire wealth? I want more money and wealth for the sake of feeling more secure in my lifestyle. I want to demonstrate affluence, living in a way that reflects my attraction to beautiful things. The wellbeing of my family and friends is associated with my desire for money; I feel great pleasure to offer to others, the things that have brought happiness and contentment to me.

I will be patient with myself. I don't have to do everything well. This life is about discovery and exploration, not being perfect at everything the first time or ever for that matter. Some things come naturally but some don't and that's okay. The process of discovery ultimately deepens the meaning of life. I will enjoy the process of discovering new things about myself and the world around me. There is something infinitely beautiful about life's imperfections. They demonstrate the uniqueness of people, places, and things. Without differences, there is no variety and without variety life is dull and mundane.

I will get there and the process is a great joy. I am grateful. Truly Thankful!!

Self-love at its core is maintaining loving thoughts about yourself. Consistently being kind and patient and affirming ourselves. All thoughts and words are affirmations, so we must create and maintain positive affirmations as the building blocks for an amazing life. Because, if the building material is substandard, then the integrity of the building is compromised.

I will not guilt or shame myself into or out of any situations. I will instead take responsibility for my actions, understanding that I can choose another way. I can correct mistakes and decide to do things differently. Sometimes taking responsibility may require apologizing to myself or others. Of course, self-correction is a part of the process. It is noble, not weak.

I love myself and everything I need to know is revealed to me. It never comes too late. As I ask the Universe, it is given to me. I have everything I need, my self-love and empowerment keeps me in alignment with the love and empowerment of the Universe.

I will slow down and listen to direction from my inner self. I respect my guidance and opinion. Self-connection is important and I will no longer neglect this very important relationship. It is the most valuable relationship that I have.

I will use my imagination and visualization to create the most amazing life. I ask my imagination to expand and expose me to other-worldly adventures. I deserve these wonderful experiences. I want to observe the good in the Universe.

I will praise and reward myself for being a positive force in the Universe. My thoughts and emotions are allies, not enemies as I create an amazing life. I don't have to earn a space in this world. Wellbeing is my birthright and all that I desire comes to me because I am an extension of Source energy. I am the governing presence of God in the earth, with value and purpose.

Day Three Reflection

_____

_____

_____

_____

_____

_____

_____

_____

_____

_____

_____

_____

_____

_____

_____

_____

_____

_____

_____

_____

_____

Shunta L Wilborn

Day Four: An Encounter with My Younger Self

"We each possess the ability to engage in self-healing through contemplation and self-analysis."

— Kilroy J. Oldster,

A close friend recently suggested that my emotional baggage - as it relates to relationships and love - is a result of doubt and fear, of being 'let down'. I wasn't sure I agreed completely with the assessment at first but I thought it was worth exploring. Yesterday, I stumbled across an article that discussed the emotional effects of being disappointed. Remembering my friend's comment, I decided to read it.

As far as I could tell, the author's intention was to answer the question, 'Where did the pattern of being let down really come from?' I felt curious about her take on the subject, so I read further. According to Cassidy X, the author of the article, childhood is usually where you are "taught... that disappointment might await you." She suggests that "when you pinpoint the core origin of the pattern (of thought) and neutralize the frequency, you stop attracting disappointment." With nothing to lose, I decided to explore the idea.

As suggested in the article, I closed my eyes and remembered back to a time when I first felt insecure as it relates to money, and when my expectation of being let down by people (especially men) began. Back to a time when I felt powerless to choose my own destiny. I learned to associate feelings of uncertainty and powerlessness with safety and love. Honestly, remembering was a bit unsettling initially. What didn't come easily, was how to comfort the frightened little girl I encountered. My younger self didn't appear as I remembered. I knew exactly how she felt but she seemed fine, happy even. She was an expert at masking her pain.

I imagined kneeling to her eye level and offering her a loving embrace. I told her that I wanted to begin healing mentally and emotionally and explained that I needed her help. Lovingly, she agreed. I knew she felt some responsibility for the experience and I told her that none of those situations are her fault. I assured her that she made decisions based on all that she knew in the moment, which wasn't much... if anything at all.

Without assigning blame to anyone, I offered my younger self healing and poured love into her fragile heart. I explained that she was now free from the burden of feeling worthless, inadequate, fearful, or unloved. I told her I loved her deeply and have decided to be uncompromisingly kind and patient with her. I promised that I would not scold or ridicule her for any of the choices we made then or now. I assured her that great things are in our future and all that we've ever wanted is sure to come. In the meantime, I released her to be a little girl. I encourage her to go play and explore her world without the responsibilities and concerns of adulthood. I asked her to discover her interests and experience every moment without regret.

Don't be afraid Shunta, you are smart, capable and worthy to experience your wildest imaginations.

Throughout the day, I imagined my younger self playing, reading and laughing; doing it all with a smile so vibrant even the July midday sun would take notice. Witnessing her happiness shifted something deep within me. At this point, I am not sure what it all means but I am definitely sure it is significant to healing the past wounds of my heart.

For that, I am grateful...

Shunta L Wilborn

Day Four Reflection

Day Five: Transformation

"The most important journey you will take in your life
will usually be the one of self-transformation.
Often, this is the scariest because
it requires the greatest changes, in your life."
— *Shannon L. Alder*

If I had to describe the experience of my self-love affair in one word, it would be transformative. The most cathartic experience so far has been letting go of my tendency to look outside of myself for love and acceptance. After reading an article, 'A True Path to Love' by Deepak Chopra, I decided to think more about how I want to experience love in a relationship. More than superficial deeds or kindness, I want to explore my opinion on the personal characteristics that make a good companion. What would someone who loves me want 'for me' rather than 'from me'?

My exercise this afternoon is to create a list and demonstrate those loving characteristics towards myself. I have decided to date myself, say loving things, protect my heart, buy myself flowers, and even pleasure myself if necessary. I don't consider the latter inappropriate, as I once would have. After all, isn't that one of the things a lover does? Well I intend to do it all because I deserve to be loved by someone who has no intention of hurting me in any way. Who better for the job than yours truly?

I've also had to remind myself a time or two that the next 25 days are not about anyone else in any way. I don't have to justify my feeling about anything with anyone. No one needs to be there for me, I have committed to doing that for myself. I am not inclined to figure out anything for anyone else, No one. It feels really good to take full responsibility for myself and my own needs. Figuring out what makes me happy and when I stumble upon something that does not, discovering the root and loving myself through to healing feels amazing. Each day and night, I have learned something new about how and why I experience love the way I do. This is an exciting time of introspection and I look forward to discovering the woman that is Shunta.

I love you, Shunta. You are a one-of-a-kind treasured asset. You are valuable above anyone's ability to understand. You are a stunning beauty, but you are so much more. Maybe tomorrow, I will make a list of my amazingly wonderful attributes and remind myself of them all day long. Oh how I enjoy doting on myself. It's both unfamiliar and natural. Whenever I am tempted to solicit validation from someone else, I remind myself that this time is about me and that whatever I need, I will provide for myself. While I enjoy companionship, it is important now to teach myself that I am never alone because I always have myself. I am never without love, because I love myself more than anything or anyone. As a priority, I will no longer sacrifice my wellbeing for the sake of others. That's a pretty tall order for me, but I am up to the task because I am worth it!

Today's Exercise: What are the things that I would want a lover to do?

- Demonstrate that I am a priority
- Share a deep connection, emotionally and spiritually
- Give and receive honesty, even when things are hard to say or hard to hear. Provide me with assurance that he will always be honest and have my best interest at heart
- Provide fidelity, that we maintain a sex life that is exclusive
- Present creative expressions of his love
- Make me laugh, a lot!! Even when we face less than desirable situations, I want a man that can make me laugh (and I can do the same for him)
- I want a love that is purposeful to more than just the two of us
- I want a love that is secure. I want chemistry. I want fire and passion

- I want an amazing lover
- I want a person, wealthy and ambitious, kind and generous, smart and creative and resourceful
- I want to make magic!!!!!!
- Oh and….HANDSOME!!!

Thank you God, I am eternally grateful for the journey!!

I think I will also do mirror work tomorrow. This should be fun. I expect that it will be the best day so far. Each one seems to get better than the last. I am so excited.

Day Five Reflection

Day Six: Magic in the Mirror!

The journey isn't about becoming a different person.
It's about loving who you are right now.

— Suzanne Heyn

It has been an extremely emotional day today. Spiritually heavy, I've felt the need for guidance from my inner being more than usual. I have a lot on my plate, but which direction to take professionally has been a burning question lately. I've been feeling unsure and even a little confused about the next step to take. Honestly, I don't even know if there is a next step. Something within is whispering its time but I feel paralyzed, afraid to misstep, like I'm standing in the middle of a field able to go in either direction but the idea of taking the smallest step one way or the other terrifies me.

Feeling overwhelmed I decided to do what has never failed me, have a candid conversation with Source. Only, without all of the drama. Absent the asking, begging and crying, and all of the other emotional manipulations I've put myself through in the past. It's a learned behavior, from a system that teaches us that God has to be coerced into getting involved with what we care about, that we have to perform for His attention. Thankfully, I've realized that all of those 'spiritual antics' are unnecessary and don't make me any more or less worthy to be heard by God. Besides, I just don't want to do that anymore. It feels foolish. I know that Source is loving and that I have access to infinite wisdom, intelligence, and universal resources. What I need is not hidden from me and I don't have to beg for it. I need simply to, "ask and it is given".

The answers that I seek are always waiting to be discovered. They are as anxious for me as I am for them. Understanding that there is mutual benefit here, is the first step to the success I desire professionally and in life in general.

I am curious to understand why desperate energy shows up when I think about the things that I want. There seems to be a longing that drains the excitement from life, like a low frequency feeling that's weighted and strapped. I need to know that I can take care of myself. In doing so, I must take 100 percent responsibility for the choices I make and the ones I don't. Honestly, I feel like I have never lived independent of someone else's desires and opinions. Always, either needing or wanting someone there to validate me in one way or another. Where has that come from? Where did I learn that it is someone else's responsibility to meet my needs?

I want to feel satisfied with life and I am not so sure I do presently. Dealing with the raw emotion of not living the life I deserve is no easy thing to acknowledge, but now is the time to face it and live my truth. In search of that truth, I had to go back to the time when I decided settling was an option.

What I found was not at all what I expected. I encountered my 8 year old self who was very wise but equally naive to her circumstances. She was accustomed to being in adult situations but had no idea that she was ill-equipped to navigate through them. This little one was a master at disguising her feelings so I was a little lost on how to comfort her. Honestly, she appeared to not need it. She knew exactly how to mask the pain that was always there with grown up words and a resilient 'I'm okay' attitude. Just like my 45 year old self, she was scared out of her mind, unsure as to what the next moment would bring or if she had what she needed to make it through. We have always been savvy enough to talk the talk and resourceful enough to at least appear to walk the walk. The authenticity, the foundation that a good life is built on, was never solid if it was even there at all.

Even though she appeared to be okay on the surface, her eyes told a different story. They were full of pain and there was fear behind them. She seemed to be 'ready for whatever' but I knew that she was fragile and should be handled with care. As I spoke to her kindly, she began to open up emotionally. She told me that secretly she was falling apart. Making 'big girl' decisions was hard, and she had no idea what to do next. She was skilled at putting on a happy face but rarely was it authentic, always feeling that things could go really wrong at any moment. From her childish perspective, she said she knew things would be okay somehow but the space between the problem and the answer felt like a minefield.

In that instant, I realized that that timid little girl still thrives inside of me. I told her that I share her fears of not having or being enough. She needed to know that along the way, there would always be someone there to guide her to safety and love. So did I.

I assured her that together we would fulfill our purpose. We wouldn't always know exactly how, but along the way things would get easier. We'd be careful not to allow disappointments to shape our view of life negatively.

I lovingly hugged her and asked for forgiveness for the missteps that we would make during our journey. She cried but then she smiled. She was the most beautiful she had ever been in her life. She was relieved to be a little girl again, No longer trying to navigate this adult world without the life experience or resources. She was free to play without care. Free to grow and develop on her own terms. Free to just be a little girl, something she had not been given the opportunity to be.

The journey into my childhood brought to the surface emotions I believed had long been resolved. I thought I had forgiven my abuser but I realized that the abuse was still influencing how I showed up in the world. Specifically, it triggered my insecurities regarding intimacy and sexuality

An honest evaluation of my relationships uncovered a willingness to relinquish responsibility for my sexuality. That's not to say that I feel powerless when it comes to intimacy, but I haven't cultivated the courage to explore or push boundaries. Primarily for fear of being judged in one way or another. Like most abuse survivors there are triggers and ideology as it relates to sex that are not aligned with healthy sexual experiences. For me, it shows up as under-stimulation because my assessment of sex has been that it's nasty or bad or just not what 'good girls' do.

I don't mean to imply that I have not enjoyed intimacy in my adult relationships but ultimately it's been colored by shame and guilt rather than excitement and desire. It is amazing how your first sexual experience builds the framework moving forward. I didn't get to choose or feel the anticipation of my first kiss; I didn't feel the excitement of having a crush or falling in love.

To heal and move forward, I re-visited that complicated part of my childhood. Remembering wasn't as easy as I thought it would be. I have done my best to block out that part of my life and deliberately revisiting that pain was uncomfortable to say the least. I didn't know if it would take me back to a dark place, but offering a safe place for my young self, was worth the risk. Bravely I sat with the emotions, feeling them deeply, and when I felt ready, I began to talk to the little girl within me that felt powerless but unsure why.

I told her that she was in no way to blame and that she didn't need to carry the burden of that pain anymore. I offered to take on the pain because I am better equipped to handle it and she hesitantly gave it to me. I released her from the obligation to hold it all together, and she felt a huge weight leave her shoulders. Her happiness was contagious.

I suggested we have a 'do over'. Together, we would go on a journey of self-love and emotional healing. First we would learn to love the self deeply, unconditionally, and uncompromisingly. We would establish life on our own terms. Then we would love someone romantically, someone that we chose. We would have a crush on him. Then, we would fall in 'like'. We'd get to know him and maybe we would love him enough to 'do it' LOL!

She liked that idea and decided to take me up on it. What she liked most was that she was free to be a little girl with little girl problems and little girl solutions. No more grown up stuff. She beamed as she felt the heaviness of responsibility leave her being. I told her I was glad she felt happier and

I apologized for not having this visit sooner. She forgave me. We hugged and she skipped off with her balloon into the sunset. She's free and it feels amazing.

Today, I have chosen mirror work as my daily exercise. I am not sure if I want to create a script, just let the words flow naturally, or some combination of the two. Luckily, I have a few hours to figure it out.

In the meantime, I think I'll take some time to center myself. It's been an emotional morning but worth every tear. It is only day six and emotionally speaking this journey of self-love has been the toughest, yet most rewarding thing I've ever done. I am so excited to see what the following days will bring!

———

The mirror exercise was extremely insightful. I decided against writing a script or affirmations. Instead, I looked directly into my own eyes and spoke from my heart. The words came effortlessly and I committed to discovering the truth about who I really am. I apologized to my inner child again for the things that she had to endure over the years and committed to loving her deeply and unapologetically. My words were bold, firm, and sure. Absent any fear, I promised to take care of our needs and set her free to explore life on her own terms. To find what she's passionate about, to discover her gifts and find her way to profound happiness. We have settled for second best and now it's time to live the life that we choose, the one that we create based on our own desires. I set her free to love and learn, to expand and create; she is free to develop the gifts that will shift the consciousness of this world.

I have been created with purpose and I intend to fulfill my purpose, powerfully. I commit to healing the hurts of my inner child so that I am free to create without the fearful influence of what was forced upon me. Without feelings of helplessness, living life on my own terms. I reminded myself of how valuable I am and promised to never forget or treat myself in a way that doesn't demonstrate worthiness. I am the most important person in my life. I will not esteem anything over my decision to love and put myself at the top my list of priorities.

Day Six Reflection

Day Seven: 10 Guidelines to Self-Love

You can't hate yourself happy.
You can't criticize yourself thin.
You can't shame yourself worthy.
Real change begins with self-love and self-care.

— *Jessica Ortner*

Day Seven already.

I awoke this morning in a loving mood, it feels likes freedom. So much so, I have adopted freedom as my mantra today. Simple yet powerful!

Today I am free to let go of limiting thoughts and beliefs. Free to love myself and others. I am free to laugh loudly and feel deeply. There is no need for me to explain it to others because it's none of their business.

I know what I want and exactly what to do. Divine intelligence guides me in the realization of my goals. I have decided to give up criticizing myself and others. It is an exercise of self-hatred in either instance. I am okay exactly the way I am and so is everyone else. My focus today is on being the best I can be and experiencing love and peace in its highest form. Letting go of every boundary, I will reach for the fullest expression of myself.

I am connecting with the treasures inside me and I intend to use them for the greatest benefit to myself and others. What I am developing inside myself is needed by the world. I am worthy of this amazing gift. Starting with myself, I will share my ability to empower and give inspiration, to live my own best life. I am committed to developing and refining my gifts

Shunta L Wilborn

so that they provide influence on a global level. Before today, I would not have been able to think of myself on such a scale, but self-love has expanded my vision. It has empowered me to consider myself capable of any task and every desire. No matter how small or large, I have the ability, the intellect, and the power to create in its fullest expression.

I have escaped from the prison of my own judgement, free from the need to have others validate my opinion. I've decided to explore thoughts that I once held off limits to myself. Taking the world's stage was a desire that I've contemplated but never really imagined myself expressing. Now the idea of sharing my gift feels natural and sure to manifest itself in divine and perfect timing. Why not me? I am worthy and wise. I trust my future to be satisfying and amazing!

I want to share the guidance I've been given for achieving self love and a successful life to as many as possible. Life has encouraged me to show up for myself in a powerful way and I intend to start now. It is not important to make quantum leaps forward, the smallest actions toward love and its fullest expression is equally as powerful.

I am certain that everything I need will show up. There is no need to manipulate any situation, this is a useless act and never accomplishes anything lastingly positive. Actually, manipulation is probably a leading cause of stress and fear. It validates that I don't trust the Universe to deliver all that I need to be healthy, happy and prosperous. As a divine being I attract what I need. It flows to me powerfully and effortlessly. Joy and happiness are the center of my world and everything that I desire flows from this truth. Self-love, self-worth and self-esteem are the foundation of my joyous experiences. I've created a safe space to discover, develop, and express all that I am.

My exercise today is to listen to Louise Hay's audio, "Guidelines to Self-Love" and make a few notes.

Louise Hay - Guidelines to Self-Love

1. **Stop Criticizing Yourself & Others:** Criticism is negative thinking in action. It is the highest form of self-hatred. When we focus on the negative qualities of other people, we are allowing negative thoughts to enter into our subconscious, ultimately resulting in increased negative circumstances in our own lives. The more you criticize, the more comfortable your mind becomes with negativity and the more this starts to spill over into other areas of your life. Before you know it, you've become a 'Negative Nancy' and life is a self-fulfilling prophecy.

   Choose to invest your time in your own personal growth, instead of channeling energy into negative thoughts about yourself and others. Decide instead to speak positively about yourself and others. Change the dynamic of your inner conversation. Affirm yourself and others freely and often. Boast about your accomplishments. Replace the habit of speaking about yourself in negative terms. As you affirm yourself and others, you will feel more confident and positive. The more positive you are the more powerful you are!

2. **Don't scare yourself:** This makes things worse. It makes small situations seem insurmountable. Fear is all about thought perception. Make your thoughts your best friend. Befriend thoughts that nourish and support good and positive experiences. Fearful worry is a misuse of your imagination. Replace scary thoughts with kind and loving ones and plant them in your subconscious. These thought seeds will grow and will soon dominate your way of processing your world. You are supported by the Universe. Choose and express balance, harmony, and peace in your thought world.

3. **Be gentle, kind and patience with yourself:** Talk to yourself the way you might talk with a small child. Use kind words and select thoughts that complement joyous experiences. Don't scold yourself. It doesn't work. Affirm what you already do well and remind yourself that you can learn to do things in a different way. You are smart. Trust your inner wisdom. Listen to your own

guidance and trust it to be there at all times. Life unfolds into positive and fulfilling experiences.

4. **Be kind to your mind:** Self-hatred is simply hating the thoughts that you have about yourself. When your inner conversation is negative, don't scold or think badly about yourself. Be grateful that you have the ability to replace or change it. Soothe yourself with kind words. Use loving affirmations and create definite positive statements that build you up rather than beat you up. Don't equate a bad thought with being a bad person. Thoughts are only energy, they are not who you are. They can be either released or transmuted. Try to identify the root of the negative thought and lovingly recreate new ones. Love your mind.

5. **Praise yourself:** Praise builds up your inner spirit. It is a means to creating a good life for yourself, even if you don't think you deserve it. Praise is a means to build self-worth. Find things that you do well and use them to change what you feel and believe about yourself. We are all doing our very best. Affirm yourself boldly and often.

6. **Support yourself:** It is important to build a support team. No one accomplishes worthy goals alone, not even self-love. Find a support group or team. If you can't find one, start one of your own!

7. **Be loving to your negatives:** Negative patterns are created to fulfill a need and at some point, they worked. Release them with love and allow a new, more loving way of being, to replace the negative. You can choose new and more supportive thoughts. Use positive affirmations to change your life for the better. Lighten up. Don't take yourself so seriously. Trust the process of life and be willing to change. Release old negative beliefs and replace them with ideas. Know that you live in limitless light and joy. All is well!

8. **Take care of your body:** Offer yourself the best level of health possible. Learn about health and nutrition. Find exercise that you enjoy. Discard bad habits and create healthy ones. Appreciate and listen to your body. It will tell you what it needs. It is resilient. Make the best choices with regard to nutrition. It is the fuel your body needs to heal and regenerate itself. Good nutrition is an act of loving yourself. Speak lovingly about your body. Create an

environment of healing. Imagine the body that you desire and trust the Universe to bring to you all that you need to manifest it.

9. **Mirror work:** Look at yourself in the mirror and declare, "I love you". At first, it may seem unnatural but push past any resistance that you have to speaking lovingly to yourself. Look into your own eyes and tell yourself whatever you need to hear to heal past hurts. Do it often, it will get easier.

10. **Create for yourself a set of basic beliefs: (*These are mine*)**
    - I love myself deeply, unconditionally, and without compromise
    - Things are always working out for me
    - I always get what I want. Only good awaits me at every turn.
    - I am an expression of Source energy, able to create the life that I desire
    - I am divinely protected
    - I am deeply fulfilled
    - The Universe supports and assists me. It conspires for my wellbeing.

Day Seven Reflection

_____

_____

_____

_____

_____

_____

_____

_____

_____

_____

_____

_____

_____

_____

_____

_____

_____

_____

_____

_____

_____

_____

Day Eight: A Strange Dream

*"You may say I'm a dreamer, but I'm not the only one.
I hope someday you'll join us. And the world will live as one."*
— John Lennon

This morning I had a strange dream. It is almost embarrassing to share. Normally, I wouldn't but my journey of self-love has emboldened me to open up in way that I wouldn't have dared to before now. This journey has opened up a space for me to be completely transparent, understanding that my experiences are perfectly orchestrated by the divine. Everything that happens is for my best benefit and advantage. It works for my good and sharing it may be exactly what someone else needs to clarify confusing circumstances as their path unfolds before them.

This dream was a bit unsettling. I remember being in a home (I'm not sure if it was my residence) that I had never occupied in my physical experience. I started noticing that there were bugs – roaches - showing up in the rooms of house. My aunt Nancy was there with me and a couple of other people who I can't identify. The number of roaches began to increase. They were popping up everywhere. Of course, I was completely disgusted and decided to get rid of them with bug spray, only I could not find any. Meanwhile, the bugs were multiplying. Big ones, little ones, adults and babies. Surprisingly I was not afraid. I just wanted to exterminate them.

When I awakened from the dream I felt curious about what it meant. I was certain that this dream showed up as a message to me. Honestly, I was a bit nervous about finding out. I tried to resist the urge to research its meaning but felt compelled to find out. There was a bit of nervous energy as I began to read about what this dream might mean for me.

The first article was a little ambiguous in nature so I moved on. The next one was just as confusing as the interpretations were contradictory, providing both positive and negative interpretations for the similar details. I am not experienced at dream interpretation but a gut feeling encouraged me to dig a little deeper. The next couple of articles were straight forward and what I learned both surprised and excited me. It appears that these disgusting bugs are a good omen. They signify longevity, tenacity, good financial fortune, renewal and new birth. Later, I learned that the details of this type of dream are important as the smallest detail drastically changes is meaning.

As I focused to remember as many details as possible, the reddish color of the bugs stood out in my mind. I have shared below the interpretation that I settled on. Needless to say, the description of the little critters in my dream has changed my feelings. I dreamed about riches rather that roaches. I am so excited to see what great fortune, renewal, and rebirth awaits me. Of course, I immediately bought a lottery ticket!! Oh what will I do with SO MUCH MONEY!

Dream Interpretation:

To dream about seeing reddish-colored cockroaches is a symbol of benevolence. You could soon receive a lot of money as a gift from a person close to you or from someone you would least expect to give. In any case, you would feel lucky and thankful for being the recipient of this touching act of generosity. The number of reddish-colored cockroaches you see in the dream is proportional to the amount of money you will receive. That is, the more cockroaches, the larger the amount. (dreamlookup.com)

Daily Exercise: Tonight during bath time, I listened to another of Louise Hay's YouTube videos on relationships, entitled "Power Thoughts on Love and Relationships." In it, Hay explored ideas she discovered to attract romantic relationships. She introduced her lecture by stressing the importance of improving the relationship you have with yourself.

According to Hay, "when you are happy with yourself all of the other relationships that you have improve as well. A happy person who loves himself is very attractive to others. If you are looking for love then you need to love yourself more."

She shared many of the exercises that I have created for myself over the past week as a means to strengthening your self-love relationship. As I listened I smiled and thanked the Universe for confirming that I am on the right path.

Here are some other ideas that she suggested:

1. **Demonstrate self-love:** Pamper yourself. Treat yourself with flowers and diners. Surround yourself with things that please you, things that you would expect a lover to do, do for yourself. Make a list of the characteristics that you would like your lover to possess. Be willing to become those things if you aren't already. Be sure that your list is not fear based; they are shallow and don't work. Take time to develop your 'love list'. Create it as if the list will manifest. Then drop it and move on.

2. **Tell yourself, "I love you":** Look in the mirror and declare your love for yourself. Say your name, "Shunta, I love you. I really love you." Do it often! It is extremely important not to criticize yourself. Speaking kindly and lovingly as you affirm that you are loved.

3. **Create a loving mental atmosphere within and around yourself:** Think of sharing love, approval, and acceptance with yourself and everyone that you meet. Work to stay centered, calm, and secure. Fulfill your own needs so as not to appear clingy or needy. A needy person operates in fear and pushes people away. It is a demonstration that you don't think that you are worthy of what you want. Be open and receptive!

4. **Invest in your personal healing:** Let go of negative thoughts about love and romance and surround yourself with things that reflect a loving energy. Be willing to do the work to heal your past

hurts. Be patient. There is no need to hurry through the process. Give yourself time to heal. Stay focused on yourself. No whining or blaming other people. You are 100% responsible for your own healing. As much as you can, enjoy the process.

Day Eight Reflection

_____

_____

_____

_____

_____

_____

_____

_____

_____

_____

_____

_____

_____

_____

_____

_____

_____

_____

_____

_____

Shunta L Wilborn

Day Nine: Who Can You Trust?

"To be trusted is a greater compliment
than being loved" — *George MacDonald*

During meditation this morning, the idea of trust surfaced. A quick evaluation of the loving support team that I have left me beaming with gratitude. I consider myself blessed that I have several people in my life that I can depend on to show up, no questions asked. People whose opinions I trust and value deeply. Then the question arose, 'Do I trust myself?' Honestly, the thought caused me a bit of anxiety. I would like to say that the answer was an immediate and resounding "yes!" But it wasn't. Because I want this journey to be life changing, I realize I have to be completely honest with myself, even when that truth makes me uncomfortable.

Trust for me, is a matter of honesty and loyalty. At the heart of trust is thinking and taking action in one's best interest consistently, not necessarily to the detriment of yourself or others but to the highest degree possible without self-betrayal. Trust requires a connection that is divinely inspired. It is much deeper than the friend or familial bonds that are broken and mended easily and often. Trusting behavior demonstrates reliability, truth, and strength.

I turned my attention back to my thoughts about my personal level of trust. I consider myself a trustworthy person but my answers to these questions made me reconsider that truth. Can I really rely on myself to demonstrate trusting behavior towards myself? Do I always have my best interest at heart or have I decided that prioritizing myself is selfish? Am I personally reliable or do I flake out when things get difficult. Do I keep my confidences and promises or do I betray myself by agreeing to do things that make others happy, even when I have no desire to do them?

Before now, I may have been disappointed at the notion that I am not who I thought. Fortunately, this discovery excited me. I am eager to take the opportunity to develop and redefine love, trust, and transparency for and with myself. Trust is the foundation of love. Without it, there can be no lasting or meaningful connection. I've decided to use my time today building trust with myself. Making decisions that express deep intimacy. I will take care of what I love. I will put it first. I will treat it well. I will make decisions that are in my best interest. I intend to fulfill these promises and much more!

Shunta, I promise:

- You can trust me
- You are safe and I will protect you
- You are important to me, you are my priority
- I will not betray your confidence. Who you are is completely safe with me
- I will keep my promises to you. Even if it means others might be disappointed. I will no longer disappoint you for the benefit of others
- I am a safe place for you to rest and be yourself
- I love you deeply and I intend to do whatever it takes to ensure that you never question this truth

Day Nine Reflection

_____

_____

_____

_____

_____

_____

_____

_____

_____

_____

_____

_____

_____

_____

_____

_____

_____

_____

_____

_____

_____

_____

Day Ten: Guidance & Intuition

"When you trust your inner guidance and begin moving in the direction of your dreams (aligned with your individual gifts) you will be cloaked in an armor bestowed upon you by your guardian angel."

— Charles F. Glassman

Today, I've realized my focus is shifting. Things that were once of great concern for me, no longer have a place of priority. I am learning to trust my inner guidance. Within me are all the answers to all the questions I have. I realize that if I follow my intuition I can avoid the feelings of doubt or confusion that paralyze my progress. My instincts are heightened when I trust and love myself. Guidance is and always has been available to me but my lack of self-love was resistant to its powerful flow. Letting go of resistance has proved to be the most meaningful decision that I have ever made. I trust my ability to make the right choices and no longer need anyone to validate my opinion. Finding comfort in someone else no longer serves me in a positive way.

I choose to live free from the destructive behavior of trusting anything or anyone that feels 'off'. My intention is to live the best expression of myself through the guidance of my inner self. From every situation, I expect only good. Regardless of how it appears to me physically, all things work for my greatest advantage. I trust myself.

I live beyond all limitations, whether my own or someone else's. I create my own experiences; I get to decide. There are no conditions that will hinder my progression towards what I desire. Of course, there are obstacles to overcome but my desire will always create a path through or around them. Nothing stands in my way. I am a physical expression of Source and I intend to live from this truth. Every resource of the Universe is available to me. This world is programmed for my benefit and advantage and I am grateful.

The relationships in my life are a gift to me. Every person has come or left to give to me what I needed in the moment. Some lessons were more easily received than others but all are equally valuable. I lovingly thank each person for what they have graciously given me. Reflecting on my relationships has shown me that every person offers something uniquely beautiful. It is interesting how we all fit perfectly together. Even those who are no longer actively a part of my life. The lessons that they taught are useful to the experience that I am living now. I now understand that not all relationships are meant to be forever. My new practice is to enjoy every moment that we have together and to lovingly let them go when it is time for them to leave. I will function in all of my relationships from a position of power. Any neediness that I've demonstrated in the past was a result of my lack of self-love and self-worth. I release the need to cling to the presence of anyone. My connections are mutually desired or lovingly blessed and will release to their highest good. I am worthy of meaningful and healthy relationships!

It feels good to let go of what no longer works. I respect my ability to evaluate my circumstances in a healthy way. What is no longer fulfilling can be lovingly released. I am free to feel the glorious satisfaction of every joyous moment. There is no price to pay for my happiness. Letting go of past hurts and negative beliefs are the catalyst to my life of freedom. No more blame! I am a strong, powerful, intelligent woman. I accept myself and take 100% responsibility for my choices.

Day Ten Reflections

_____

_____

_____

_____

_____

_____

_____

_____

_____

_____

_____

_____

_____

_____

_____

_____

_____

_____

_____

_____

Shunta L Wilborn

Day Eleven: Making Changes

There is nothing rarer, nor more beautiful,
than a woman being unapologetically herself;
comfortable in her perfect imperfection.
To me, that is the essence of beauty.   *~ Steve Maraboli*

Developing self-worth is critical to successfully increasing self-love and finding my worthiness has been an act of healing. Not only has my relationship with myself enhanced, but I've noticed a change in how I interact with others. Honestly, I don't care about what they think and need as much. This may sound off putting I know, but I am no longer willing to jeopardize my happiness by co-creating a chaotic environment.

Even my conversations are changing. Recently, I engaged in a few not so pleasant conversations that didn't end as I would have liked them to. Typically I would have reviewed every word wondering if I had said something offensive or hurtful, trying to make sure I didn't do anything wrong and trying even harder to relieve myself of the uncomfortable emotions I associate with conflict. While I certainly don't want to go around mistreating people, I've realized that I don't have any control over how my words are interpreted. I've determined that my intention was not to be hurtful and I lovingly let it go.

Somewhere along the line, I learned that I needed to esteem others' feelings above my own. Now I know that that is untrue. I am worthy of being understood, receiving compassion, and having my point of view considered by both myself and others. People have only reflected back to me how I feel about myself. If I don't consider myself worthy, others will behave in a way that confirms my thoughts as true. Fortunately, I have the ability to change how I present to the world. I am deeply loved and I intend to demonstrate it in every experience.

Deep at the center of my being is a calm resonance. From this place of peace, I project my inner desires into the Universe. The love that I have for myself is the foundation of all of my relationships and all that I do. Everything is affected and I am different in the best way. This is only day eleven and how I process the world around me has already changed dramatically. Deep self-love and acceptance is mirrored to me by my relationships and circumstance.

I say yes to my greatest expression of life. I deserve to receive as much as I am willing to give. Only, I no longer give without expectation. I expect that life will bring to me good and abundant experiences. The best and greatest advantages are mine to enjoy, not because I've given to others but because I have discovered my worthiness. Loving me creates an atmosphere of fun, excitement, and exploration. It promotes mutually loving and satisfying relationships.

All of my needs and desires are influenced by how well I love myself. Past thoughts of limitation no longer have power over my present and future. What I believe about myself is my reality. I believe that I am safe, protected, loved and supported by the Universe. The Universe is focused through me, creating my desires from its infinite resources. There are no limitations on my ability to choose or re-choose. Nothing is fixed or final. I can unlearn, undo, let go, and re-evaluate anything that is not working, to my advantage.

I AM WORTHY!

Day Eleven Reflection

_____

_____

_____

_____

_____

_____

_____

_____

_____

_____

_____

_____

_____

_____

_____

_____

_____

_____

_____

_____

_____

_____

Day Twelve: Impoverished

Whoever has will be given more, and they will have an abundance. Whoever does not have, even what they have will be taken from them. *(Matthew 13:12)*

It's no secret that what you believe about yourself directly influences your level of self-love, self-worth, and self-confidence. Changing the old beliefs that no longer serve you in a positive way changes everything, it really is the magic of life. The process of making these necessary changes and asserting the power of self-love is simple, but not easy. First you have to be willing. It's natural to say you want to free yourself from limiting fears and doubts but often these fears and doubts are a deeply rooted part of your identity and being without them feels vulnerable.

I've decided to take some time to evaluate what I really believe about myself. In a general sense, I believe that I am worthy of love and respect. I acknowledge and accept abundance, creativity, protection, and support as my birthright. Discrepancies surface when I attempt to marry belief with actions. I realized that my decision making wasn't at all aligned with what I say I believe; my actions and interactions do not consistently demonstrate someone who is powerfully living according to her own convictions, someone confidently living her best life without regard to someone else's acceptance or approval.

During meditation this morning the word *impoverished* surfaced in a strong and uncomfortable way. When I am spiritually open, I don't like to introduce negative words. Actually, I was more than concerned because my attempts to bless and release the word had not been successful. Thinking that it might be meaningful to this journey, I decided to look this word up. The definition included words like *bankrupt, penniless, destitute, beggar,* and *ruin.* Because those aren't words that I ever associate with myself or my circumstances I knew this word had come to teach me something significant.

I released my resistance and accepted its presence; I befriended it and asked it to share with me, what it wanted me to know. *Impoverished* suggested that I take a look at my thought life. I followed its direction. Here are a few of the questions that it asked me to answer and explore:

- When you think about success, do you think about increasing the level of success that you have already or do you consider it something that you don't yet have?
- Do you appreciate the beautiful home that you have or do you long for the things that are missing?
- Do you rejoice in the life that you experience now or are you focused only on new desires?
- Are you thankful that money flows to you easily and grateful that your work is not hard and you are free to live the life you choose?
- When you affirm yourself, is your dominate intention to change your current experience or stand in the truth of who you really are and expand?

The final question:

- Shunta is your thinking impoverished?

I consider myself to be a positive person and I believe that positive affirmations make a huge difference for me, certainly shaping how I experience life. Consciously, I manage my thoughts and I choose them carefully. I accept that my emotions are my indication that my thoughts are either in or out of alignment with my desires. When I recognize that there is an imbalance, I quickly bring my thoughts back into alignment with the good that I desire.

Considering these questions forced me to evaluate my unconscious beliefs. Regrettably, I had to acknowledge that on an unconscious level, my thinking has been impoverished and I accepted this as an invitation to go deeper. The intention here was less about 'what' I think and more 'how' I think. My thinking - even when my intention is positive - is primarily focused on what I don't have and what I want, rather than the good that I do have in life. Life mirrors back to you who you are; Life gives to you more of what you bring to it. The scripture says, "Those who have much will get more, and those who have little…even what they have will be taken away" makes sense now. My way of thinking was impoverished, and without the gratitude for what I have.

Thankful for this revelation, I've started to appreciate my surroundings and all that I have. While I want a higher level of professional and personal success, I acknowledge that what I have achieved feels fulfilling and purposeful. Grateful, I understand that more success will show up for me. I am always at the right place at the right time and I am supported abundantly. I want a bigger home and given the fact that where I live now is so nice, nicer is surely inevitable. My home is filled with love and those who enter its doors find warmth and loving experiences. My home is beautifully furnished and provides shelter for me and those whom I love most. Every relationship that I have matters; each one is unique and offers fulfilling experiences. Deeper connections are a natural evolution in this life that I live which is a prosperous and loving one. This life wants to give to me more of the good that I have, and not more of what I have failed to recognize.

Thank you '*impoverished*' for showing up to teach me this valuable lesson. An ancillary lesson: there is never a need for me to be fearful. Everything comes for my greatest benefit.

Day Twelve Reflection

_____

_____

_____

_____

_____

_____

_____

_____

_____

_____

_____

_____

_____

_____

_____

_____

_____

_____

_____

_____

_____

_____

Day Thirteen: Self-Talk

Talk to yourself like someone you love.

— *Brene Brown*

The most important decision on the journey so far has been the one I've made to address my inner conversations. What I believe about myself is directly influenced by what I think and say about myself, to myself. Somewhere along the line, I've learned to criticize and scold myself unknowingly accepting that exposing and highlighting my mistakes would empower me to do better. This was not true, it made me less confident and less trusting of my decisions; humiliation only leads to shame and guilt.

Recently I read an article about an African tribe that practices loving restoration. When someone does something wrong they take the person to the center of the village where for two days, the entire tribe surrounds him and recounts all the good he has done. The tribe believes each person is inherently good and their mistakes are only a cry for help. Instead of punishment, the consequence for misdeeds is to be reconnected with your good nature. It sounds to me like this tribe has figured out how to live in harmony with each other.

I have made the decision to never criticize myself again. It is not a reflection of love and the Universe will yield to me what I project, multiplied. If evidence of love is what I wish to experience in this world, I must also demonstrate it in my relationship with myself and others. Speaking unkindly about others is then a reflection of how I feel about myself. When I find myself being critical or judgmental of the people around me, I have to take a deeper look at what I am feeling about myself. My relationships function as mirrors for me, showing me everything that I am.

Shunta L Wilborn

Speaking kindly to myself with love and compassion is an expression of self-respect and leads me to deeper levels of love. When I hold myself in high regard I treat myself well. I won't destroy my self-confidence with hurtful and judgmental words because self-love requires that I see myself as worthy, deserving, and competent. This is not to say that I excuse myself of responsibility when things go wrong. Actually the opposite is true. When things are not going well I turn my total attention inward. I consider what I have done to create the situation, and evaluate how or if there is something that I need to correct it. If changes need to be made, I open myself to guidance from my inner being. Prayerfully, I ask to understand what I haven't before and try to consider how I might bring the gift of who I am to the situation. When there is nothing that I can or should do, I bless the circumstance that is beyond my control and release it to its highest good.

I trust my connection to the Universe as it is my guidance. I am the governing presence of God in the earth, a spark of Source. The Universe is always listening and supporting my thoughts so how I speak of myself is reflective of my divine identity. It is to my advantage and the advantage of those around me to live, think, believe, and take action from a loving place. I am empowered by beliefs about myself and they can be a catalysts to change life circumstances, literally shifting energy flow.

Improving my self-image through self-love has changed the way I observe life. More easily, I notice the perfection along with the imperfection of life. I acknowledge that there are injustices in the world, suffering and inequality. Often these challenges seem insurmountable, but they are not. Becoming the change you want to see is the best way to overcome overwhelming feelings. Healing your own life is the first step to healing the world around you; you cannot share what you have not yet experienced.

Criticism and judgment does not change anything and while there is some benefit to conversation, conversation is not the solution. Many issues are a reflection of shadows, the dark places in the hearts of men. Only love heals the hearts of men and shining that light will bring about change. Love is light and self-love is the light that shines brightest!

Day Thirteen Reflection

_____

_____

_____

_____

_____

_____

_____

_____

_____

_____

_____

_____

_____

_____

_____

_____

_____

_____

_____

_____

Shunta L Wilborn

Day Fourteen: You just made that up!

The difference between a mountain and a molehill is your perspective.

– Al Neuharth

Today, I had an opportunity to demonstrate self-love in a very practical way. A close friend texted me a question that I started to over think on. I gave an answer but soon after, I began to wonder if there might be a hidden meaning to the question, one slightly demeaning in nature. Honestly, I considered the question a bit disrespectful. I wondered if there was a more to it and the question was a lead in to a deeper conversation. My mind tossed around scenarios that were increasingly insulting. While it was likely a question with innocent intention, the situation was quickly snowballing.

Thankfully, before I delved too deeply into my negative thought pattern, I reminded myself of my 30 day commitment of self-love. I reminded myself that this was not a time to complicate my thought life. I had promised myself to focus only on me. Whatever my friend's motivation, it was not important. Self-love reminded me that I am worthy, confident, and powerful. Someone else's intention, good or bad, was of no consequence.

I kindly explored why my thoughts followed this negative pattern. Why were my expectations of disappointment and slight? A loving thought suggested 'It is you, Shunta'. I agreed but asked my inner guidance to tell me more and realizing there was much to learn from this situation, I listened intently. My inner conversation was no longer focused on the intention of the question, but why I had been willing to create such a negative circumstance over it. I accepted that I had created this problem; within minutes, I had turned a simple question into a mind battle.

My inner guide reminded me that no one else has the ability to think for me. I get to decide what things mean. It is my perspective that determines how I feel about any situation and I can use the power of thought to support or disappoint my joy and happiness. Every situation comes for my highest good if I choose.

In that moment, I completely understood how we create our own reality. With my own thoughts, I had created chaos. The Universe was simply mirroring to me my belief system.

Where had I picked up this destructive behavior? Why was it important for me to scrutinize another's intentions toward me? I had clearly prepared for an attack where there had been no credible threat. I'd completely made it up.

As I considered these questions, I realized that it is my habit, I've learned to be suspicious of people's intentions. But why? The good news here was that while I had created this unwanted experience, I could just as easily create a positive one. I shifted my inner conversation. Because I get to write the script of my life, I decided to make the exercise work for me. Releasing the need to blame anyone else for my feelings, I decided to reconsider the question and from my new perspective, I decided to accept the question as a compliment. Like magic, the entire situation has turned for my good.

Perspective changes everything; as my mind changed, the situation changed. It was at my direction that the question transformed. I'd had no more input from my friend and the question had not been clarified. I was not given more information, I just decided to embrace myself with love and compassion. Without judgment, I acknowledged that I had given meaning to things that were not there, which was unfair to my friend. I took responsibility for allowing my thoughts to take a negative turn.

Self-love reminded me that life reflects back to me what I think and believe. I questioned out loud, "Shunta, what do you want to have supported by the

Universe?" I want love, respect, kindness, positivity, excitement, laughter, happiness, light heartedness, and friendliness mirrored back to me. In this moment I decided that I will redirect my thoughts to love in every situation. I trust myself and the Universe!

Day Fourteen Reflections

Day Fifteen: Finding My Power

You do have a story inside you;
it lies articulate and waiting to be written
behind your silence and your suffering.

— *Anne Rice*

My deepest desire is to be reunited with my life's purpose. Today, I am asking the Universe to support me in re-aligning with my truth. While listening to an audio of self-love affirmations, I was inspired to open my heart to love and live from a position of power. I am freeing myself to move into new and satisfying experiences.

I will not abandon myself. I am not sure why the negative feeling is so strong but I have committed to experiencing self-love and I will not walk away. It does not matter what happens. I will gently bring my thoughts into alignment with my new belief system. I believe that I am worth the effort. Love – especially love for myself - is my new way of living in this world. I am in love with me. I cherish myself and I promise to give whatever it takes to be whole.

I never want to depend on anything or anyone for my happiness. All that I need is within me and I can access it at any time. I can change any situation that arises so I am never stuck. I trust myself and the Universe to deliver everything that I need. If I need peace, or money, or resources, I'll ask for it. The answer is always yes. I promise to never spend another moment feeling needy or experiencing lacking. Those feelings are not my reality.

Even if I have to do it through the cloud of tears, I will give to myself every opportunity for love, joy and happiness. It is always up to me. I can wallow in sorrow and sadness or I can connect to the infinite source of eternal love and peace. I choose love for myself and those around me.

Negative thoughts will not take root in my mind. My thoughts are clear and positive. What I experience in life is an amazing expression of the powerful being that I am.

Thank you God for reminding me of who I really am in this world. I am worth loving and that love is without condition.

I am not limited by any circumstance. Every universal resource is mine. I choose happiness, kindness, love, excitement, heath, wealth, and passion. I am feeling much better.

Day Fifteen Reflections

_____

_____

_____

_____

_____

_____

_____

_____

_____

_____

_____

_____

_____

_____

_____

_____

_____

_____

_____

_____

_____

_____

Day Sixteen: No More Drama

Today, I've been feeling a little funky. I woke up to the sickening feeling of anxiety charged with worries about my marriage, finances and success. Even though I was able to soothe myself, I still felt discouraged as defeating thoughts crept into my mind. I got a little down on myself because I know better than to allow negativity to occupy a space in my consciousness for any length of time. After I had taken as much of it as I could, I asked my angels to help me. Typically I would include all the drama of crying out to God, literally, and asking for help in my most pitiful and sorrowful way. Not this time.

All the drama was unnecessary at this point. I decided no more. With trust and conviction I prayed and asked God to help me, declaring that negative thoughts are no longer acceptable to me. They are detrimental to my future happiness so I asked for help in releasing them. After a few minutes I could feel the tension leaving my body. A smile emerged and peace settled into my body.

I wanted to gain clarity on why my thoughts had shifted so dramatically and clearing the clutter in my bedroom helped me to clear the clutter in my mind. For some reason, rejection has been a recurring issue for me. When I start to feel rejected in any way I run to my shell for protection. Unwittingly, this self-alienation creates deeper feelings of rejection, and as I shut myself off so that I don't feel the pain of the loneliness created is just as painful. Why is this such as issue for me? I don't want to activate the energy of rejection but I do want to heal it so that it does not affect my future any longer.

God, please show me where I've picked up this belief that I am not worthy of the love I desire. Show me how to heal it. You have given me all that I need to live powerfully. This journey towards loving myself unconditionally has provided a space for me to heal and grow. I intend to magnify only the good.

What I want is to awaken to the truth of who I really am. Absent ego and personality, I want to acquaint and express the infinite eternal being that I am. Life has brought me to a place where I must examine my fears and voice what they are, acknowledging them as illusions that I have allowed to control my thoughts and consequently, my actions.

Fears about my marriage, abandonment, success, money, and love have kept me trapped in a self-imposed prison. I've decided to shine light into that dark cell and I discovered there is nothing there. Nothing.

The hardest step was the first. But once decided, I stared fear in the face and said, "Bring it". I resolved that whatever happens - even my worst thought - just happens. When I realized that my thoughts were creating my emotions, I was set free. My dread filled thoughts had created the shadows and empowered imaginary monsters who now controlled me. It was all in my mind. Without the energy of my thoughts the fears died. Unwittingly, I had been its life energy.

What am I aside from my desires for money, success, physical pleasure, attention, and love? I am love, energy and passion, a spark of the Divine. I am a creator, with infinite wisdom, intelligence, balance, and harmony and I want to live from that reality. I want a true awakening to the god force expressed as Shunta. My ego is resistant to this reality but my desire for authenticity is much stronger. I want to experience how it feels to live my bliss, discovering in every moment what it means to be me.

At this point I want to live free from the control of mental manipulation. Thought is simply the manipulation of energy, a form of interpreting energetic forces so that it can be manifested and physically utilized. Thought is our way of creating the realities we experience. Only much of the time, it feels like my thoughts think me rather than the other way around. I spend so much time trying to manage my mental self, making every effort to keep my thinking positive and aligned with my desires. It's true that today's thoughts create tomorrow's experience. I often wonder if I will be satisfied with my future.

Self-love has shifted how I think, but life is much more than thought. We are human beings. Our being-ness is the essence of the life force that we are. It is our individual expression of God. I cannot rely solely on my thinking to give me direction. It is as limited as my past experiences, absent inspiration from the divine. My thoughts will always follow my personal, ancestral and environmental forms. I realize that in order to live a free and joyous existence I have to connect with my inner being for guidance.

Higher levels of living require a transcendence in thought, the going beyond of what we know, embracing the unknown, and accepting our personal divinity. Once we have achieved this higher vibration everything that is not in alignment with our true nature will remove itself from our experience. Creating reality in this way is not only personally fulfilling but shifts the consciousness of everyone you encounter. It is creation at its best.

Shunta L Wilborn

Day Sixteen Reflections

Day Seventeen: Transcending Thought

"Love transports mortal beings to the existential plane of spiritual eternity transcending the emotional, mental, and physical limitations of an inaccurately perceived finite existence."
— Ken Poirot

Self-love is really a return to self. Not the self that represents the beliefs, material possessions, and identity we accumulate in mindless incessant thinking but the self that is like God, mysterious and eternal, free from mental labels. It is awakening from learned unconsciousness and expressing your true divine nature. Self-love is not acting lovingly towards yourself, it is not even making decisions or thinking in your best interest. Those things are simply a demonstration of self-love. Actual self-love is acknowledging, accepting, and expressing the truth of who you are, unapologetically.

During my morning meditation, I experienced a moment of true thoughtlessness. It was a momentary glimpse at life through the lens of infinite intelligence. A disassociation from all that I consider myself to be, without judgement or criticism. I disconnected from my expectations, worry, fears, accomplishments and relationships. Only me without thought, present in being, not doing or desiring. I experienced a level of peace far beyond anything I've ever known. Who I really am revealed itself in the most powerful way, far beyond what my best thoughts could ever create.

It was a moment of elation. I realized that there is really nothing I can't do, have or be. In fact I already am those things, although resistance has not allowed me to experience them. False ideas like guilt, shame, unworthiness, and inexperience have obstructed the flow of love, empowerment, infinite wisdom and intelligence.

My willingness to fearlessly let go of myself created a pathway to every possibility. More incredibly, it was the realization that I *am* every possibility. We are unbounded potential, free to explore every option or not, it is completely our choice.

There is no way to have a full existence without thought and used properly, it is key to limitless experiences. My mind is creative in nature, able to manifest whatever it can contemplate, however there is much to experience beyond thought. What you are able to know through intellect is a tiny fraction of what actually is. In the state of thoughtlessness, infinite creativity, balance and harmony, love, ideas and organizing power flow freely. Mind and thought are simply the doorway. Beyond that door is an energetic sea of consciousness that creates and sustains all that is. Whatever you desire can be created when non thought directs your thoughts.

Day Seventeen Reflection

_____

_____

_____

_____

_____

_____

_____

_____

_____

_____

_____

_____

_____

_____

_____

_____

_____

_____

_____

_____

_____

_____

Shunta L Wilborn

Day Eighteen: Ego & the I AM Presence

"Only the truth of who you are,
if realized, will set you free."

— *Eckhart Tolle*

I began re-reading "A New Earth" by Eckhart Tolle a couple of days ago. It has reminded me of how much ego controls human behavior. Tolle defines ego as identification with form, fueled by the madness of incessant thinking. As I took in his words, I realized that my ideas of going beyond thought to experience the essence of self or self-love has been spot on.

Tolle explained that the ego is neither right or wrong, good or bad, it just is. I am not sure if he considers ego something that we should rid ourselves of but he encourages *presence* as a means to awakening to and letting go of it.

Maybe letting go is the only way to manage the maddening mind patterns that fuel the ego. Certainly, the transformation of consciousness requires a dis-identification with it, which according to Tolle, is the main purpose of his book.

Tolle suggests that awareness of the 'I AM' presence is the beginning of awakening to life and is where transformational shifts begin. Most of us are asleep, predictable, and identified with things or forms that are fleeting. Our thoughts are the same as they were yesterday or culturally the same as our ancestors. We have been thinking the same thoughts and involved in the same activities and making the same decisions for decades. Talk about being stuck! Every moment is evaluated through the lens of future happiness. For so many, it is unthinkable to find the present moment satisfying.

Connecting with my truth, my I AM consciousness, has opened me up to understanding love and trust in a completely different way. I am finding that trusting myself is the most important element of this journey. Why? There is no love without trust, trust is the truest definition of the word love. I must give credibility to my own intuitive guidance or I will second guess everything that I am. Trusting that my power is the magic that I have been searching for, has shifted the reality that I create.

I understand that I have created everything that is my life. Painful experiences are a result of not being aware of or disallowing my power. Life is lived effortlessly when we recognize the ego structure and let go of it without judgement or resistance, living consciously. Those who live this way are often called 'lucky' or 'blessed'. Fortunately, we are all connected; we are all a part of this infinite I AM presence.

How do we awaken to this awareness? How do we plug in? According to Tolle, we simply transcend thought. Some call it meditation, quieting the mind and allowing presence to flow through. When you stop following the mind's desire to think, this will happen automatically and without effort. I've practiced meditation for years now. Personally, mindful awareness feels a little different. Rather than making it "a thing", I accept it as my authentic state, my conscious awareness.

The key for me is understanding that I don't have to think or affirm my way to presence. Affirmations are transformative but they are not necessary for feeling my presence. My being-ness does not require an explanation, it need only be acknowledged. I acknowledge that in moments of stillness thoughts or words only dilute my power. There is no label that can identify my essence so I accept the powerful feelings as me.

Wisdom is not what we think it is. Before now, I would have defined it as deeper than information, not necessarily intellectual but definitely akin to knowledge only found on a higher level of understanding. Now, I know that wisdom is actually truth. It is a deep intuitive knowing of the truth.

Trusting the truth of who you are is the beginning of all wisdom; without it there is none.

How does all this relate to self-love? Love is your most authentic state of being. It is the 'I AM' that is God. Jesus said, "I AM, the way the truth and the light." That is love. Your "I AM" consciousness is the way to whatever you desire, the truth of who you are and the light that shines and illuminates the dark shadows.

We have to acknowledge our 'I AM' being-ness, beyond thought, belief, mindset, or even religion. We are spiritual beings created in the image and likeness of the Creator. So who we are has to be defined through this lens. The degree to which we neglect this truth is the degree to which we err.

It has been interesting to recognize how often the ego surfaces. It is equally amazing how quickly it will relent once acknowledged. According to Tolle there is nothing else that is needed. Ego, finding your identity with form - whether mental, physical, or emotional - and presence, identifying with your 'I AM' consciousness cannot co-exist. If you are aware that what you are experiencing is a demonstration of the ego, you cannot in that moment be completely identified with it.

The more we awaken and shine the light of love into the shadows, the less power the ego has to influence who we are. True happiness, self-love, and self-worth happens when we define Self through our connection with Source. Anything else is temporary and false.

Day Eighteen Reflections

_____

_____

_____

_____

_____

_____

_____

_____

_____

_____

_____

_____

_____

_____

_____

_____

_____

_____

_____

_____

Shunta L Wilborn

Day Nineteen: Lights, Camera, Action! What role do you play?

"Authenticity requires a certain measure of vulnerability, transparency, and integrity."
— *Janet Louise Stephenson*

Today I had an 'A-Ha' moment regarding how rare it is that human beings are truly their authentic selves. We are more often than not playing a role, be it parent, lover, friend, employee, co-worker, or otherwise. There are so many masks we wear, it's hard to know where one ends and another begins. It's surprising that anyone knows who they really are. The idea of not measuring up has pushed us into the prison of make believe and fear won't allow us to break free.

We even enlist our emotions to solidify this role playing. We talk ourselves into and out of emotional states based on what we need in each moment, anything to get the attention that makes us feel identified with one label or another.

I decided to strip away every label and feel my authentic self. At first it felt unnatural. I completely identify with my position as mother and wife, friend and daughter. Who am I if not those things? If not a black woman, or pretty girl, then what? Without my desires or plans, who am I exactly? After all, don't we spend a life time trying to become all of these people? Shouldn't we identify with them? Don't they add value and purpose? I imagine 'enhance' is a more accurate term here, but is this such a bad thing? Aren't we all working to enhance ourselves?

Most would answer a resounding 'yes' to those questions. The problem is that all we define ourselves by is fleeting constantly changing. Unstable! The roles that we assign ourselves are just that - roles. The people in our lives don't need play acting, they need to experience who we are, not how well we can pretend. We put on a happy face when we are sad and act as if we have it all together when we are really feeling lost and confused. We grin and bear it when what we really need is to ask for help. We demonstrate that it is more important to appear happy than to actually be happy.

When we expose exactly who we are, our relationships are authentic. Isn't that what we really want? A true connection, a life lived with someone who is real no matter how flawed? And aren't flaws merely differences? In other words, aren't they just a demonstration of our uniqueness? Isn't that what gives us value - what makes us a one-of-a-kind treasured asset? I think so.

Shedding roles and finding identity in presence - not in things - is the gateway to finding your value. The fear of judgement and criticism keeps us locked in a prison of our own creation. Self-love, including trust and worth, are keys to unlocking the cell doors.

Day Nineteen Reflection

Day Twenty : Self-Acceptance

"Wanting to be someone else is a waste of the person you are."
— Marilyn Monroe

Accepting who I am has freed me from mental and emotional cages. I don't want to throw away this powerful gift of self-love in an attempt to live out some recycled illusion created by someone else's mind. From childhood, we are indoctrinated with ideas of who or what we are supposed to be, and conditioned to live our lives based on the traditions of our families. We learn to consider our abilities through the limitations or accomplishments of others. We accept a reality that society has formulated as all there is, inheriting its fears and rarely, if ever, questioning its validity.

I've noticed that my mind creations, once a fundamental part of my identity, are changing. Someone else's opinion of me is no longer important, I do not care whether others consider me successful or esteem me in one way or another. Of course I want to be liked, but admiration from others is no longer necessary for my happiness. I can't live up to idealized expectations - self-imposed or otherwise - neither do I want to. It is exhausting!

I am learning to trust my own ideas. We all have a sacred path to follow, a unique journey that complements who we are as individuals. We are not meant to follow a predetermined path, people who do are typically unhappy and rarely make an impact. Our mission as earth dwellers is to manifest who we are. That is the work that we are commissioned to do and I intend to do just that.

Because the relationship that we develop with ourselves is flawed, how we connect with others suffers. Most of what we do is a performance to some degree, resulting in relationships that are not sacred but inauthentic. Like programmed robots, we mindlessly regurgitate scripts from the character roles we play, forfeiting the excitement of getting to know ourselves through meaningful interactions with others.

During dinner, my youngest daughter Kaylon and I had a conversation about friendship. It's really interesting to hear how a 17 year old processes life. Like most girls her age she is experiencing a struggle with self-acceptance, which reveals itself in her relationships. After sharing my thoughts, she asked if I thought that she was closed to authentic relationships. I was taken back by the question but excited that she wanted to talk more about the subject. I explained that I thought so, but not for the reasons that she might expect.

Kaylon, like most of us, is only willing to expose parts of who she is for fear of being judged or criticized. She presents as perfect and protects that image at all costs, only the image is a portrayal of what she thinks others want her to be. The problem is, keeping up with the ever changing opinions of others is an exhausting task. Even more challenging is holding on to who we really are in the process.

When we conceal parts of our true nature, we rob others of the opportunity to experience who we really are. More importantly, we live fragmented, dis empowered and compromised lives. I explained to my daughter that the only way to have an authentic relationship is to be willing to share our authentic selves, understanding that our uniqueness is our gift. My only warning was to proceed selectively; not every person deserves to know you intimately.

Both of my children are remarkable and uniquely talented. Their outer beauty is undeniable but doesn't compare to what's inside. I want them both to accept and demonstrate their greatness, especially as they co-create relationships of substance . Understanding that unapologetically being who you are creates meaningful connections. Your truth not only attracts what you desire, but also people that will celebrate your authentic self. Vibrationally, we attract who we are. If we are closed and ashamed of our flaws, we will attract people that validate that position.

After our conversation, my thoughts shifted. Where had she learned to protect herself in that way? As parents, we want to project or demonstrate who we are in a positive way. Only, children are much more perceptive than we give them credit for, especially young children. Needless to say, she had learned, from me, over the years to hide her true self. She's picked up on my insecurities and accepted them as her truth.

I am hopeful that the conversations continue, so that this process helps her as much as it has me. But more than that, I am committed to demonstrating for my children self-love and acceptance. Young women need to not only hear they are worthy and capable of great things, they need to see it demonstrated in the women they encounter. If we are not careful, our fears of rejection and un-worthiness are unconsciously transferred and add to their struggle. The good news is that love, acceptance and worthiness is just as easily transferred.

We are all responsible for our own wellbeing, but it feels amazing knowing that demonstrating my personal transformation can make a difference in how my children see themselves and show up in the world. I am blessed!

Day Twenty Reflection

Day Twenty One: The Magic Power of Yes!

"Gratitude unlocks the fullness of life. It turns what we have into enough, and more. It turns denial into acceptance, chaos to order, confusion to clarity. It can turn a meal into a feast, a house into a home, a stranger into a friend."

– Melody Beattie

I say yes to this moment, exactly as it is. I don't want to change one second of my reality. I say yes to love and life and power and wisdom. I say yes to uncertainty and magic and passion. I say yes to the thoughts and ideas that have caused so much suffering for me and in accepting their truth, I have found indescribable moments of peace. I say yes to a love that is connected and full, free, uncaged, mutual, and supportive, a love that lifts me and encourages me. I say yes to loving myself and loving those who bring laughter and joy into my experiences.

My yes aligns me with my desires. It opens me up to that magical space where everything that I ever wanted lives and freely flows. I no longer resist life as it comes. It carries with it the ingredients to fully create the life that I want. Even when I am unaware, I take into me a love that is divine, one that cannot be explained or understood. It is not divided or shared with anyone else. It is mine to enjoy. The Universe experiences it as me, uniquely.

What a glorious experience. Tears of joy and excitement stream down my face as I realize that everything about who I am has shifted. I don't want anything to be different. I accept it just as it is, understanding that every moment is necessary. There are treasures to be uncovered. Life delivers only what's good and it gives to me its best. Nothing that happens is coincidental. In fact, it is synchronized. It has come for my greatest benefit because it is what I need in the moment to bring me to consciousness.

Greatness does not await me. It is now. For certain, my life is an expression of the divine on this earth and I will live accordingly. I no longer have to have anything. I am not needy. I am what I am. Presence is sufficient and in self-awareness I experience the gift of self, gloriously expressed through the eyes of Source. Why haven't I seen it before now? Why did it take so long?

The full expression of 'Me' is what I want to demonstrate. 'Me' is who I must manifest; everything else is ancillary - Beneficial perhaps, but not necessary. I empower myself to greatness. My desires create themselves if I allow it. My love increases and cannot be bound or limited by any earthly circumstance. Thank you God for revealing yourself through 'Me'. The experience is magical, like nothing I've ever known. I am completely in love with me!

Day Twenty One Reflection

_____

_____

_____

_____

_____

_____

_____

_____

_____

_____

_____

_____

_____

_____

_____

_____

_____

_____

_____

_____

_____

Shunta L Wilborn

Day Twenty Twenty : Expectations

"This is the key to life: To expect everything to be given to you from above, yet to be genuinely surprised and forever grateful, when they are. Expecting all good things to be yours, while not knowing how to take anything for granted. If there may be a key in life, this is the key."

— C. JoyBell C.

This morning I read Chapter 11 in the "Autobiography of a Yogi" by Paramahanda Yogananda entitled "Two Penniless Boys in Brindaban" The story opened my mind and heart in way that I hadn't expected. It shifted my thinking about the influence of expectation on the process of manifesting the things we want in life as well as how we experience that manifestation.

Mukunda, the main character in the book, is searching for enlightenment. Having returned home from a short stay at an ashram, he is unpleasantly greeted by Ananta, his older brother, who considers Mukunda's search for enlightenment a waste of both time and their father's money.

Ananta wanted to show Mukunda in a practical way, that life - and their father's money - had insulated him from the real world; if Mukunda was forced to rely only on the "Invisible Hand' of God to provide, he would realize how foolish his beliefs were.

Ananta devised a plan to test Mukunda's faith as well as validate his own skepticism. He challenged Mukunda and his friend Jitendra to take a journey that required total reliance on God. Ananta proposed that the boys take a day trip to the nearby town Brindaban without taking any money to meet the needs of the day or to return home. They couldn't beg for food or money, nor could they reveal their predicament to anyone. The boys were not allowed to miss any meals and they had to return home by midnight without having broken any of the rules. Everything that they needed would have to be provided by God.

Without hesitation, Mukunda accepted the challenge. His friend Jitendra was not as confident but none the less, he accepted. The boys were given tickets and immediately escorted to the train station.

During the trip, two men, assuming that the friends were runaways, attempted to befriend the boys. Wanting to help, they offered to give them both food and shelter once they all arrived in Brindaban. Mukunda rudely declined, denying that they were truants and seemed insulted at the idea that they needed any help. The men did not insist any further but imposed kindnesses once the boys arrived in Brindaban. The men summoned a horse cab for the boys that took them to a beautiful hermitage amidst evergreen trees on well-kept grounds. When they arrived, the men left the boys in the care of a gracious and motherly ashram hostess, Gauri Ma. She welcomed the boys and explained that she had been preparing for two royal patrons, who had unexpectedly changed plans. Thankful that her preparation would not go to waste, she insisted the boys stay for lunch. As they squatted for lunch, Gauri Ma, fanned the boys in Oriental fashion.

Ashram disciples passed to and fro with some thirty courses. Rather than a "meal" the boys were treated to a feast fit for royalty. Throughout the day, their needs were met in equal fashion. Far in excess of what would be required. In fact, not only were their tickets back home purchased by a stranger eager to help. They were given a bundle of rupee notes (money) as a gesture of endearment. The 'Invisible Hand" had "showed out" Lol!

As I read the passage, my eyes filled with tears and my heart with shame. I realized that like Mukunda, I have always believed in divine provision, However, my expectations have never rose to the level of royal accommodation.

Something righteous occurred to me as I read. It is only my expectation that limits or enhances my lifestyle. Mukunda believed that God would certainly provide. So much so, that he refused to allow Jitendra to take 'just in case' money from Ananta, believing that God's provision could not be outshined by anything man could offer. He expected that God would prove faithful in a SUPER natural way. Mukunda even declined help on several occasions, testing that each situation was indeed the means by which God wanted to provide.

When faced with the idea of scarcity, I always considered that things would be fine. I've known through experience that my needs are always met. Only I didn't graduate to the "according to God's riches in glory" part. If Mukunda and his friend had been given stale bread, fruit, and water, it would have been by God's hand. But they were extended delicacies prepared for royalty. Why is that? What made the difference? Expectation!

I have always trusted that I am loved, supported and protected by the Universe, but to what degree? I asked myself, 'Shunta what do you expect? How do you imagine the Universe will provide for you? Scantily or overwhelmingly? I had an awakening. When just enough is considered a miracle, if not restricted by my own limited expectation, I can experience overwhelming provision. Perpetual abundance is my new lifestyle.

Day Twenty Two Reflection

_____

_____

_____

_____

_____

_____

_____

_____

_____

_____

_____

_____

_____

_____

_____

_____

_____

_____

_____

Shunta L Wilborn

Day Twenty Three: Keeping My Commitment

"The most important person to keep your promises to, is yourself."

- Anonymous

Today has been filled with reading and reflecting. I had lunch at a local restaurant, which is a deviation from my daily trip to Starbucks to write. After reading a few chapters in "Autobiography of a Yogi", I decided to take a trip to the Barnes and Noble at a nearby mall. I didn't have anything in particular in mind to buy, I just thought a change of scenery would do me good.

My emotions were all over the place, realizing how my desire for self-love has actually guided me to a desire for enlightenment. Like bread crumbs, each book, article, and video are nuggets of wisdom, left by Spirit, guiding me to self-realization. Excitement and gratitude washed over me like waves crashing to the shore. Joyful tears filled my eyes but did not wet my smiling face; for a moment the sun and my smile were in competition. The thought of transcending my body and feeling oneness with Source overwhelmed my senses.

I couldn't fathom one reason to be denied this glorious gift – my desire would be sufficient pay. Earnestly, I decided to spend the rest of my life in pursuit of presence with God. For a few moments I felt as if I were living in slow motion.

I have to stop getting caught up in writing a book that someone wants to read, and write the book that I need to write. Not from some guru type wisdom but filled with the things that matter to me and ideas that change my mind. I know that I am filled with inner wisdom but I believe not every word has to be perfectly descriptive. Does that kind of thing even matter? Probably not as much as we think. What I need is something that points me in the direction of God's love and fulfills my desire to help.

The desire for success still wakes me up in the morning. I want to know what I should be doing. I want to provide for myself and not depend on anyone else to take care of me. I want to fulfill my purpose.

Tonight, I am rambling on but I am keeping my commitment to myself; I am reflecting and writing daily. What matters is that I don't quit on myself. I am worth the effort and God is with me to see this through. Thankfully, I have the help of my Spiritual team and they never let me down. Thank you all for diligently showing up when I need you. There is so much for me to do and I am going to exceed every expectation. I am great, I will fulfill my purpose fearlessly. In one year, my life will look completely different, my desires will have materialized. But there will still be much to do. My finances will have increased dramatically and I will be in the throes of the success I desire now. Each day, I will honor my connection with God and follow my inner guidance. Teach me, I am ready to learn.

Day Twenty Three Reflection

Day Twenty Four: Free At Last!

"In the process of letting go,
you will lose many things from the past,
but you will find yourself."

— *Deepak Chopra*

Emancipation Day! Its 9:45pm 6/27/18 and I've just decided to free myself from the thoughts that have enslaved me for about a year now. I've been tightly holding on to something that wasn't holding tightly on to me. I've been afraid to live without it, but not anymore. Maybe the very thing that I feared happening. is the gateway to my ultimate happiness. Whether this is so or not, I'm going to take the chance.

Willingly. I have discounted myself for a few glimpses of connection and conditional love. What I've wanted most is an opportunity to love and trust and connect. Somehow I thought I could develop that outwardly even if it meant compromising my inner self but not anymore. I've set myself free from the chains of expectations of anyone other than God and myself. It's scary, but I am okay with that. Sometimes you've just got to stare that lion of fear in the face and deal with whatever happens next.

Taking responsibility means giving myself a chance at real happiness. Realizing that I'm not exactly sure what that looks like is a bit unsettling but if you can't be honest with yourself, who can you be honest with? Tonight, I give myself permission to explore life on my own terms. I will not live and die without the experience of mutual love, kindness, respect, and deep connection. I will not.

Shunta L Wilborn

From this point on, I am done with the compromise. I'm not saying that things have to be my way or no way, but my way definitely has to be considered, even weighed heavily. No more, "whatever you like" from this girl. Disrespect and hurtful words are no longer tolerated here. I am a physical expression of the Divine and I intend to live accordingly.

Honestly, I enjoy being me, unapologetically and with all my quirks and moods and goofiness, with my tummy and these thick lips, I love it all! Nothing about this girl is accidental. Everything that I desire is granted to me and the Universe is happy to oblige my outlandish requests. I am grateful eternally.

This smile in my heart has been missing for a while but it has returned now, shining through and witnessed by everyone I encounter. I am not afraid anymore! I am willing to do whatever it takes to live the life I've incarnated to experience. Ooo wee! This is going to be fun!

I dreamt this morning that I pulled a creepy looking object out of my throat. At first glance it was grayish in color but upon further examination I found that it was ivory and it opened to display religious symbols. Curious to know what it meant, I did a little digging but found nothing. So I decided to do what I should have done first - I asked my inner being what it meant and the response was very reassuring. I instinctively knew that this dream had something to do with communication.

My guides suggested I research the throat chakra. They told me that I am an excellent communicator in every way, orally, written, and even in my body language. With my throat chakra spiritually cleared things would begin to drastically improve in those areas. I researched the throat chakra, and this is what I found.

> *The Throat chakra is about the expression of yourself: Your truth, purpose in life, creativity. Note that this chakra has a natural connection with the second chakra or sacral chakra, center of emotions and creativity as well. The throat chakra's emphasis is on expressing and projecting the creativity into the world according to its perfect form or authenticity.*

Another function of the throat chakra is to connect you to spirit. Because of its location, it's often seen as the "bottleneck" of the movement of energy in the body. It sits just before the upper chakras of the head. Opening the throat chakra can greatly help align your vision with reality and release pressure that may affect the heart chakra that is located just below.

The throat chakra is associated with the etheric body, which is said to hold the blueprint or perfect template of the other dimensions of the body. It's an important reference point to align the energy through the whole chakra system

Source: https://www.chakras.info/throat-chakra/

Day Twenty Four Reflection

Day Twenty Five: What Are You Focused On?

"Sometimes we focus so much on what we don't have that
we fail to see, appreciate, and use what we do have!"
— Jeff Dixon

Developing my authentic self is the most important thing that I can do for both myself and the people I love. The world needs my unique gifts, not a dressed up clone of someone else. I am an expression of God and it matters that I show up in the world and demonstrate the Divine in my own way.

Tonight I listened to an Abraham Hick audio on YouTube about focusing on what is satisfying rather than the things you want changed. Abraham explained that enjoying the satisfying parts of life is what puts us in the receptive mode. I've noticed that over the past few weeks I have become less worried about what is not working and more appreciative for what is working. Even in my nightly journaling. I don't always know what to document but I've realized that doesn't matter. This time is about me and no one else. Maybe it will inspire others and maybe not. The purpose here is to remind me to love and trust myself. It has been a time of discipline and commitment. I have kept my promise to myself, which is a huge deal.

I cannot remember a time that I have followed through for a full 30 days on a promise to myself. If this was for someone else, I would have done whatever it took to make it happen. Well I deserve the same effort. My word to myself is much more sacred than to others. Breaking personal promises trains the subconscious to believe that you are not trustworthy. It promotes behavior that devalues who you truly are.

Honestly, I am so proud of myself. I did it and I love it! I have proven that I matter to me and it completely affects how I treat others and how I allow them to treat me.

Yesterday, at Barnes and Noble, I grabbed a book of the shelf on Zen meditation. Carefully flipping through the pages, a few topics grabbed my attention: thoughts, posture, and breathing. A quick read of a few of them provided a few new techniques I decided to include during meditation this morning. I'm glad to report, they made a huge difference.

What made the biggest difference was not trying to stop the thoughts. The book suggested that I allow them to come and to be released like waves. I felt more connected to my environment, more in control. I connected with my spirit guides and angles more deeply. This time is not for instruction or guidance but for the fun of the interaction. This life is what I decide it will be. I get to choose, but wait, I don't have to choose. I want it all!

Day Twenty Five Reflection

_____

_____

_____

_____

_____

_____

_____

_____

_____

_____

_____

_____

_____

_____

_____

_____

_____

_____

_____

Shunta L Wilborn

Day Twenty Six: It's All Vibration

"If you want to find the secrets of the universe, think in terms of energy, frequency and vibration."

— Nikola Tesla

Today I decided to have brunch at local restaurant and the weather was perfect so I opted to sit on the patio. It was an absolute delight. I ordered the bananas foster french toast and eggs scrambled with cheese and bacon. The chef outdid himself and frankly, so did I.

My waitress was very polite and attentive which made for an exceptional experience. I was happy to take in this moment as an expression of my desire to live on my own terms without regret or fear.

While waiting for my meal I decided to read more of "The Autobiography of a Yogi." So far, the book has opened my mind to a level of spiritual wisdom that seems unbelievable.

This particular chapter, 28, was Yogananda's account of the life and reincarnation of one of his favorite students, Kashi. During an interactive question and answer session with Yogananda, Kashi inquired about his future. The young boy wanted to know if his destiny would be strict devotion to God or if he would enjoy a traditional life including a wife and family. Without taking time to temper his words, Yogananda blurted out, "You will be dead soon". Needless to say, they were both shocked and aggrieved by the abrupt and unexpected prediction.

Accepting that his guru's words were prophetic, Kashi pleaded with Yogananda to find him when he reincarnated. Initially Yogananda refused, not wanting to think too deeply about his beloved Kashi's death, but later he lovingly relented to his young protégé's consistent request.

Soon after, Yogananda had to take a business trip. While he was away, Kashi's father visited the school and against his wishes took Kashi home for a visit. While away, the boy ate contaminated food, contracted cholera and died. Heartbroken, Yogananda rushed to Calcutta where the boy's parents lived. Grief stricken, he over reacted and accused Kashi's father of murdering Kashi. Yelling, "You killed my boy!" Realizing he'd been wrong to take Kashi away, the boy's father shamefully apologized.

Yogananda's love for Kashi and his pledge to find him after his death weighed heavily on him.

Here is where the story gets interesting…

To find Kashi, the yogi employed a secret yoga technique of broadcasting and tuning, similar to the functions of a radio. He "broadcasted love to Kashi's soul through the microphone of the spiritual eye, the inner point between the eye brows. [He] intuitively felt that Kashi would return to the earth soon." Yogananda unceasingly broadcasted his call to Kashi's soul until it responded. He knew that the slight impulses from Kashi would eventually be felt in his fingers, arms, and spine.

"Using upraised hands as antennae, [he] often turned round and round, trying to discover the direction of the place in which, [he] believed he had already been conceived as an embryo. For six months, Yogananda practiced this technique. Eventually, he received feedback as sensations tingling through his arms and palms as currents that translated themselves into overpowering thought in the deep recesses of his consciousness. Kashi was calling! Overjoyed, with up raised arms he followed Kashi's magnetic soul whispers to a couple's home who was indeed expecting a male child. Yogananda informed the couple of his reason for the unexpected visit. Astonished, the father and mother believed him and named the child, who bore a striking resemblance to, Kashi." As a teenager, the reincarnated

Kashi contacted Yogananda and shared his longing to follow the path of a yogi. He was eventually accepted as a disciple of a Himalayan master.

I was intrigued by the idea of using the mind and body as a means for broadcasting and receiving signals. The technique doesn't seem foreign or farfetched. We are vibrational beings so it seems natural that our souls would be able to communicate, whether or not we are in a physical state. His mention of upraised hands was at first, a bit weird until I related it to church where we are taught to raise our hands to the Lord. It never occurred to me why we do that and more importantly, why it feels uplifting when we do. When we raise our hands, they become receivers for spiritual energy. Not only can we project thought with our minds but our extremities can be used as broadcasters or receptors as well. Sometimes I wish I had someone to throw these ideas around and try them out with. It seems amazing that we can align with the vibrations of others and create magnetic connections. Maybe someday. Hopefully, someday soon.

Day Twenty Six Reflection

Shunta L Wilborn

Day Twenty Seven: I Get To Choose

"The most important thing is this:
to be able at any moment to be free
to choose a life that makes you happy."

— ***Roy T. Bennett***

Life is a reflection of your deepest desires and fears. The Universe is gracious and it provides for us according to the thought energy we project. You are light and love as you are created in the image of God and God's desire is for your illumination of the god self, perfect in Spirit and in form. My inner being spoke these words as I subconsciously asked the questions 'what is life?' and 'who am I?'

Today has been a particularly emotional day. I'd like to say it's hormonal but that's just another label we give to things we don't yet understand. Fed up after half a day of self-inflicted emotional crisis, I decided to meditate and ask how to let it go.

My inner guides reminded me that I was creating my sadness. My thoughts are mine to choose and think. No one is deciding, thinking, or feeling but me and if I want something different, there are an unlimited combination of ideas to choose from. I was liberated!

I remember the feeling that I had yesterday during meditation. For the first time ever, I felt completely connected to everything. There was no separation in any way as I realized that everything I wanted is energetically connected to me so vibrationally calling for it is all that is needed.

Right now I want joy, freedom from the nagging thoughts of self-pity. Immediately I affirmed, I am not pitiful. I am powerful! I live as God does, in His likeness. What is that likeness? Light and Love. The Light that is me is powerfully illuminated, not dim or shadowy.

I decided to shine brightly and welcome the confirmation of my new creation. Like magic, I had fashioned a delightful feeling of happiness in my heart and mind. Not by necessarily thinking new thoughts as much as releasing the ones that were producing my unhappiness. Harmony, balance, and creativity surfaced as I opened up to beams of love that were shining to and through me.

There is no better feeling than realizing that you have the power within to create whatever you want. You don't have to settle into a bad day or frustrating cycle. At any moment, you can choose to release what does not please you and replace that with what does.

It is simply a matter of exchanging the maddening egocentric mindset for awareness. Realizing that the negative cycle of thought was only feeding ego, I shifted my attention to presence. It was immediately clear that I had almost forfeited a day of joy and bliss for gloom and sadness. I had a choice to make. I could either continue on or release it and allow the light to shine through. It was a no-brainer. The light poured in, illuminating my mind, spine and extremities. As presence filled me, I could feel the negative energy being transmuted into love.

I am thankful for my inner guidance. Grateful that the I Am presence gives only good. Life offers its best to me in every situation, all I have to do is allow it.

I LOVE MYSELF!!

Day Twenty Seven Reflections

_____

_____

_____

_____

_____

_____

_____

_____

_____

_____

_____

_____

_____

_____

_____

_____

_____

_____

_____

_____

_____

Day Twenty Eight:
Other-worldly Experiences

"It seems, something inside us persistently wants to believe in things, unexplainable by words."
— Mladen Đorđević

Tonight I contemplate the idea of self-realization. As I read the accounts of other worldly experiences - that of Yogananda and his fellow gurus - I realized that other worlds exists as real as the one we inhabit. I wonder how much of what we experience is organized or even orchestrated by our spiritual counterparts. How influenced are we by their actions, if at all?

I am curious to know how it all works. More than ever, meditation has become a point of connection to all that is. My spirit is so expansive that all things are encompassed within it. The oneness eradicates the illusion of separation. In this state, I understand life without limitation.

In his book, Yogananda recounts stories of his guru interacting with human beings who are able to occupy physical bodies at will. Some transport and send messages through mental energy. Others create whatever is needed at will. One story in particular interested me as it offered a glimpse into creation.

In the story, Yogananda recounted a story told to him involving a Babaji, a guru who materialized a palace in the Himalayas.

In tune with the infinite all-accomplishing Will, Babaji was able to command the elemental atoms to combine and manifest themselves in any form. He created a beautiful mansion out of his mind and is holding its atoms together by the power of his will, even as God's thoughts created the earth and His will maintains it…When the structure served its purpose, Babaji dematerialized it.

"As I remained silent in awe, my guru made a sweeping gesture. This shimmering palace, superbly embellished with jewels, has not been built by human effort; its gold and gems were not laboriously mined. It stands solidly, a monumental challenge to man. Whoever realizes himself as a son of God even as Babaji has done, can reach any goal by the infinite powers hidden within him…even so, the lowliest mortal is a powerhouse of divinity.

From a non-spiritual perspective, the stories are easily dismissed as delusion but I find them fascinating and I want to know more.

I accept that I am spirit, so the idea of my physical experience as a shadow performance of a higher dimension is completely plausible. This spiritual search for self-love has elevated my desire for enlightenment. I have awakened not only to love but to the power to create the life that I desire through light and love, the greatest energy powers there are. "Whoever realizes himself as a son of God…can reach any goal by the infinite powers hidden within him" What is the infinite power hidden within? It is light. En-light-en-ment; oneness with God

"Let there be light! And there was light" In the creation of the universe, God's first command brought into being the structural essential: light. On the beams of this immaterial medium occur all divine manifestation."

The law of miracles is operable by any man who has realized that the essence of creation is light. A master is able to employ his divine knowledge of light phenomena to project instantly into perceptible manifestations the ubiquitous light atoms. The actual form of the projection (whatever it be: a tree, a medicine, a human body) is determined by the person's wish and by his power of will and visualization.

I am…light!

Day Twenty Eight Reflection

Day Twenty Nine: The Sweetness of Self Love

Emotionally, these last couple of days have been a bit challenging; joy and happiness have seemed just beyond my reach. I began to wonder if the work I am doing is effective. Am I achieving the results I am after? Seemingly, I slip back into my old ways of thinking. Thank God, that once you know the sweetness of self-love, nothing less will do.

When I am not living from love, naturally life feels a bit off. My relationship with me is the foundation for every other relation. Love is my guide for successful living. Ignoring my guidance and intuition brings things to an abrupt halt. I am learning to appreciate these god given mechanisms and I am grateful that the Universe is conspiring for me and allows me to self-correct.

The beaming light of love that emanates from me attracts all that I desire and I am careful at this point to protect that. Completely fulfilled by my own love and acceptance, I enter each moment. No longer looking outside of myself for validation.

Validation for me is huge. Wanting to feel like who I am matters and is worthwhile. I've used it to feed my self-esteem, big mistake! Seeking worthiness from anyplace outside of yourself is disastrous. My confidence and esteem now naturally flow from my connection with Source and nothing else. Anything is easily accomplished when love creates the blueprint.

Shunta L Wilborn

Peace, love and joy are my natural states of being today. Feeling otherwise are only emotions resulting from a mind story, whether positive or negative. While emotions are considered by many the GPS of life, you have to be in tune with your inner being to really stay on course. Connection with inner guidance is most important and freeing myself from the well-crafted story of past hurts and resentment has freed me to connect.

So far, the most important lesson that I have learned is that I am responsible for my own emotional state. Any suffering, hurt, pain, sorrow, or tears are of my own creation. Alone, I think the thoughts, I've created the story. Yes, things have happened that are beyond my control, especially as a child. But it is my decision to nurture and empower the thoughts that continue to affect me. Only what I identify with affects me.

For example, I am not a victim of sexual abuse. The abuse happened to me and it was significant but it only affected my decision making as long as I internalized the guilt and shame. When I challenged those thoughts, things changed. Sure, it took some time to clear that energy and work had to be done but I no longer identify with it. It happened, but is intentionally missing from the story that I tell myself. I am not trying to act as if hurtful things never happened. That's likely the worst thing that you can do. I am suggesting that it is possible to disconnect from the hurtful feelings by no longer identifying with them as a part of who you are.

Healing has been an ongoing process but I am worth it. Life is as good to me as I am willing to be to myself. Excavating the treasures that are deep within has been one of the most rewarding gifts that I have given to myself. The process is simple but Lord, it aint easy. I trust the process and life to deliver good to me.

Day Twenty Nine Reflection

_____

_____

_____

_____

_____

_____

_____

_____

_____

_____

_____

_____

_____

_____

_____

_____

_____

_____

_____

_____

_____

Shunta L Wilborn

Day Thirty: There will be challenges

I'm thinking, I may need a few more days. Lol. Really it seems my deepest fears have begun to surface. Sadness continues to creep into my heart and mind and past feeling of loneliness and abandonment have been triggered. I find myself vulnerable to the idea of rejection. I am proud that I am able to choose for my best interest, no matter how afraid I am of the impending pain. I am just not sure why I have become so emotionally fragile. This life thing can get a bit complicated but I am strong and up for it. Can't give up, right?

This self-love journey didn't promise to come without some testing. After all, how do we know what we are made of, if it's never challenged? Honestly, I was hoping it would. Wishful thinking, I guess. I can say however, that it has certainly made me less willing to compromise myself and my value. It feels like the challenges are mind play. When I use the tools that I have gained over the past 28 days, my concerns melt away instantaneously.

There is a particular situation that I have struggled with over the past few months. I had slipped back into the old habit of sacrificing my happiness for the benefit of someone else. The fear of not being loved and accepted has kept me cowering and unable to find my power. I could muster the strength to say no but my heart still hurt deeply.

Emotionally raw, I knelt down in my sacred space to pray. Unable to control my emotions, I tearfully asked the Creator to help me find my power. Desperately, I wanted to find my center of peace. I prayed for strength and courage. I declared that I am not small and weak, or frightened by the thoughts that threatened my happiness. I affirmed my unconditional and uncompromising love for myself. I asked God how to exchange the tears of sadness for happy ones. I needed the strongest dose of laughter He could prescribe. *Please show me the way to joy.*

The answer came suddenly: You cannot conquer what you will not confront. 'What is it, Shunta? What are you really afraid of? Whatever it is, it cannot overcome you. You are a representation of God in the earth, now act like it. Be who you are Shunta!'

I decided to look fear in the face and say I don't care what you bring, I will not compromise myself any longer. I take my power back today. If it hurts, so what. Love is my natural state of being and I intend to live from that space and not fear.

To my surprise, the fear diminished. What had seemed an insurmountable obstacle just minutes before was reduced to a fleeting thought. For months, I had allowed the unknown to bully me into submission. Now it has submitted to me. It felt like mind play and challenging the fear made it disappear.

Thankful that the pain and fear were not without purpose, the lessons were far reaching. I realized that similar to this situation, all the other doubts and concerns that I had been dealing with were self-imposed. I decided in that moment to stop allowing fear to rob me of the amazing life experiences awaiting me. Life is to be lived and I am about to make it do what it do!

Fear is rarely necessary. Of course, there are times when danger is eminent but typically those are physical matters. The mental condition of fear is more often an emotional reaction to a mind story, a tale we've created based on either our history, someone else's opinion, or pure speculation.

Day Thirty Reflection

Bonus Day : Perfect Love
Casts out All fear!

There is no fear in love. But perfect love drives out fear...
(1John 4:18)

Today, I realized why this journey to self-love is such an important one. For the last few days I have been trying to overcome anxiety cycling through my body constantly. The fearful thoughts have come and gone and it seemed that none of the coping skills were working. Desperate, I sat alone asking Source to help me. I know that every problem has a solution and all I have to do is ask and it is given.

Fear seemed to continue to play itself out in my thoughts causing my heart to race and my body to react. I wasn't sure how much more I could take as the anxiety felt stronger and stronger. No matter what I did, I couldn't shake the feelings of dread and doubt.

Even though my body and mind were uncomfortable, my inner being would comfort me. I knew the solution was to sit quietly and wait on the answer. As I settled down to meditate, I could feel the anxiety building and the feeling of panic demanding that I open my eyes. I decided not to give in to the intrusive thoughts and trust my inner self.

As the fear subsided, I could feel the presence of Source. In my heart, I thanked her for always being there. Her uncompromising love covered me as I declared that no matter what, I know you are with me and that everything would be okay. I didn't know if the fear would come back but if it did I wouldn't be alone. Tears began to cover my face as I felt complete calm for the first time in days. I asked for the answer to calming my fears and decided to wait patiently on the answer. I didn't know when, but I knew that Source would grant me the answer to my request.

Overwhelmed with joy, I decided to take a hot bubble bath. As I settled in to my bath, I began to send out prayers of gratitude for the answer to my problem. Honestly, this had been one of the hardest experiences I had ever endured. In the midst of thanksgiving, I was reminded of the scripture "Perfect love casts out all fear". As I recited the words aloud, waves of love washed over my body. I realized that the fearful thoughts could not dwell in my mind if perfect love was there.

Then, things got even better. My inner being whispered that God's love is perfect love and self-love is God's love. Meaning that self-love comes from the Source within. Nothing outside of me is the answer. That is why the lavender oil and exercise and other tools that typically work had not. The only perfect love is that which is derived from Source. It is without condition, uncompromised, and has no limitations. God's love is pure and full and liberating. It is demonstrated as we give love to ourselves. As we know God, we know ourselves. As we experience God, we experience ourselves. I had been graciously given the answer that millions are seeking. The cure for anxiety, depression, and panic is 'perfect love', self-love is the key.

I am eternally grateful for the journey!

Bonus Day Reflection

Shunta L Wilborn

Printed in the United States
By Bookmasters